INTRODUCTION

Making pictures with nails and thread is a new, exciting, and basically simple craft requiring a minimum of skill and materials to produce the most attractive results.

This book is designed to help you whether you have had previous experience of the craft or are a complete newcomer. If you have already been introduced to this form of picture making, the book provides thirty completely new patterns from which to choose your next project. Enough information is contained in the first section, however, to enable even a complete newcomer to master the techniques involved in the making of the most complicated designs.

The basic shapes, and the techniques used to arrive at them, are so simple that after carrying out a few of the designs offered here, it would be quite possible for those interested to design their own patterns without difficulty.

Whether the completed article is made to your own design or from one of those shown in these pages, you will gain a lasting sense of satisfaction from decorating your home with beautiful pictures made with your own hands.

CONTENTS

BASIC KNOW-HOW

PATTERNS USING CIRCULAR SHAPES

There are numerous patterns that can be made using circular shapes, these are basically of three types.

1. Fill-in
2. Open
3. Divided

Fill-in method

This means the whole area is covered. Draw a circle and divide its circumference into any equal number of dots, number the dots around the circumference.

Fig. 1a

Tie on at pin 13, pass to pin 1 looping the pin, pass to pin 13, loop the pin, pass to pin 2, loop the pin and pass to pin 14, then to pin 3 to pin 15 to pin 4 to pin 16 to pin 5 to pin 17 to pin 6 to pin 18 to pin 7 to pin 19 to pin 8 to pin 20 to pin 9 to pin 21 to pin 10 to pin 22 to pin 11 to pin 23 to pin 12 to pin 24. Pass to pin 12 and tie off.

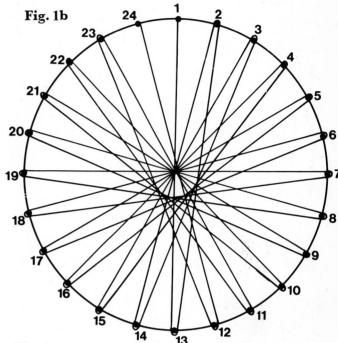

Fig. 1b

Fig. 1b

Tie on at pin 13 and thread up as in pattern 1a but this time pass the thread around the pin but do not loop it. This will result in a slightly different pattern to Fig. 1a.

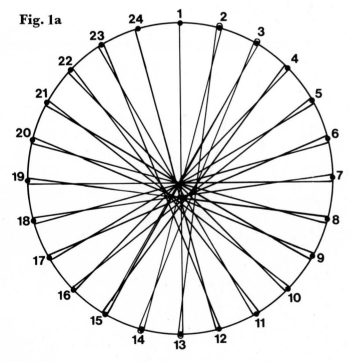

Fig. 1a

Fig. 2

Tie on at pin 25, pass to pin 1, then back around pin 25, then to pin 2 and continue in this sequence and finish at pin 25.

The sequence will read: Tie on at 25, pass to 1, 25, 2, 25, 3, 25, 4, 25, 5, 25, 6, 25 and so on in this sequence until 24, pass to 25 and tie off.

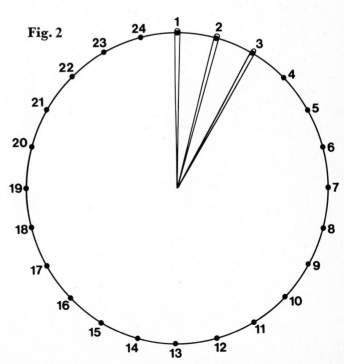

Fig. 2

Open method

This means that spaces appear in the pattern. Draw a circle and divide its circumference into either an equal or odd number of dots. If there is an even number of dots the thread must be passed on odd number of dots at a time or vice versa.

The smaller the number of pins passed at a time the larger the circle left in the centre will result.

Fig. 3

Tie on at pin 1, pass to pin 11, then pin 2, pin 12 and so on until pin 1 is reached again and tie off.

Note Small circle left in centre.

The sequence will read: Tie on at 1, pass to 11, then 2, 12, 3, 13, 4, 14, 5, 15, 6, 16, 7, 17, 8, 18, 9, 19 and so on in this sequence until 1 again and tie off.

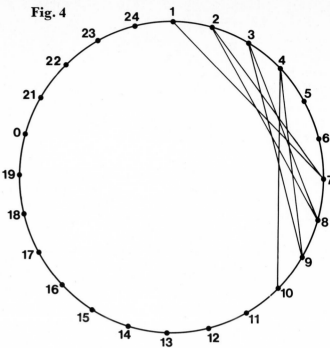

Fig. 4

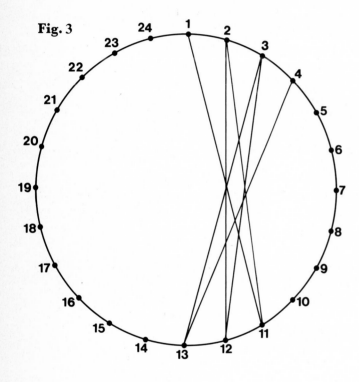

Fig. 3

Fig. 4

Tie on at pin 1, pass to pin 7, then pin 2, pin 8 and so on until pin 1 is reached again and tie off.

Note Larger circle left in centre.

The sequence will read: Tie on at 1, pass to 7, then 2, 8, 3, 9, 4, 10, 5, 11, 6, 12, 7, 13 and so on in this sequence until 1 again and tie off.

Divided method

This is composed of a circle divided for individual parts. The divided method consists of dividing the circle into any number of sectors.

The following examples show a circle divided into six sectors, with lines divided equally.

Fig. 5

Tie on at pin 1A, pass to pin 2B, then 2A, 3B, 3A, 4B, 4A, 4B, 5A, 5B and so on in this sequence until 10B and tie off.

Repeat for other five sectors.

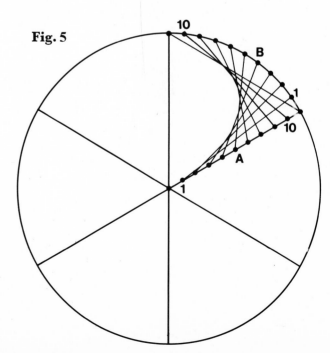

Fig. 5

Fig. 6

Tie on at 1A, pass to pin 2B, then 2A, 3B, 3A, 4B, 4A, 5B, 5A, 5B and so on in this sequence until 11B, pass to 1B, then 1C and so on in this sequence until 1B and tie off.

Repeat for other five sectors.

Note Fig. 6 is a repeat of Fig. 5 and Fig. 5 reversed.

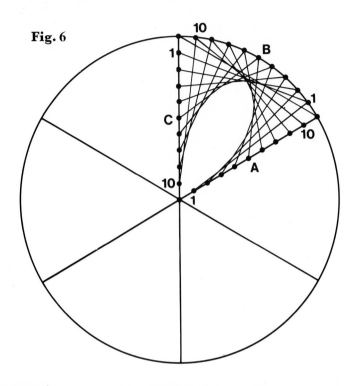

Fig. 8

Tie on at 1A, pass to 1B, then 2A, 2B, 3A, 3B, 4A, 4B, 5A, 5B and so on in this sequence until 10B, from 10B, pass to 1B, then 1C, 2B, 2C, 3B, 3C, 4B, 4C, 5B, 5C and so on in this sequence until 10C and tie off.

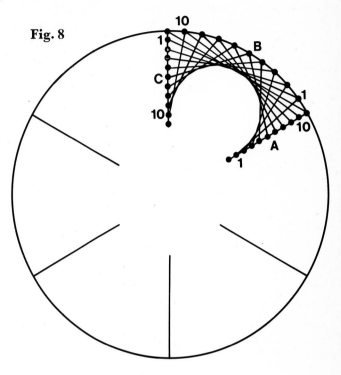

Note The Fig. 1 to 8 patterns are true for any circular or eliptical shapes provided they are treated in exactly the same way.

Fig. 7

Tie on at 1A, pass to 1B, then 1C, 2A, 2B, 2C, 3A, 3B, 3C, 4A, 4B, 4C, 5A, 5B, 5C and so on in this sequence until 10C and tie off.

Repeat for other five sectors.

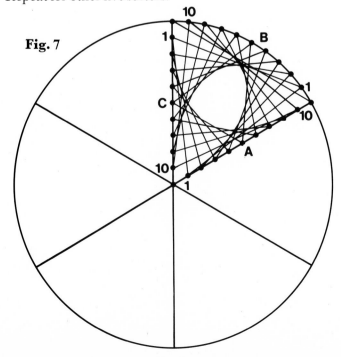

PATTERNS USING ANGLES

With angles there are three possibilities:
1. Angles of 90°
2. Angles of less than 90°
3. Angles of more than 90°

Angles of 90°

Draw an angle of 90° and divide the lines into any equal number of spaces, number the dots.

Fig. 9

Tie on at pin 1A, pass to pin 20B, then 2A, 19B, 3A, 18B, 4A, 17B, 5A, 16B and so on in this sequence until 1B is reached and tie off.

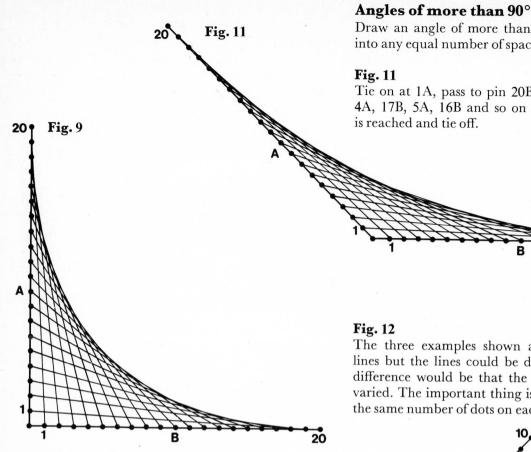

Fig. 11

Fig. 9

Angles of more than 90°

Draw an angle of more than 90° and divide the lines into any equal number of spaces, number the dots.

Fig. 11

Tie on at 1A, pass to pin 20B, then 2A, 19B, 3A, 18B, 4A, 17B, 5A, 16B and so on in this sequence until 1B is reached and tie off.

Fig. 12

The three examples shown all have equal length of lines but the lines could be different lengths, the only difference would be that the curves would be slightly varied. The important thing is that there is at all times the same number of dots on each line, as in Fig. 12.

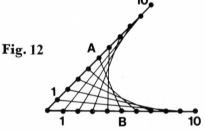

Fig. 12

Fig. 13

The lines used to form angles need not meet at one point, they could be spread out as shown in Fig. 13.

Angles of less than 90°

Draw an angle of less than 90° and divide the lines into any equal number of spaces, number the dots.

Fig. 10

Tie on at pin 1A, pass to pin 20B, then 2A, 19B, 3A, 18B, 4A, 17B, 5A, 16B and so on in this sequence until 1B and tie off.

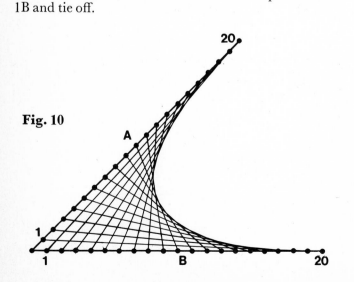

Fig. 10

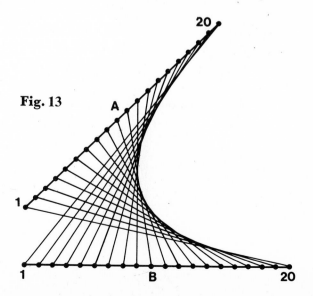

Fig. 13

PATTERNS USING PARALLEL LINES

These fall into two categories.
1. Fill-in
2. Open

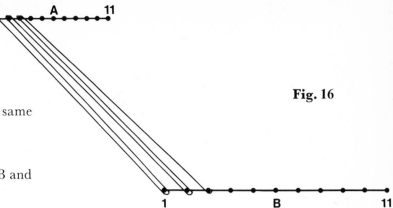

Fig. 16

Fill-in method

Draw parallel lines and divide them into the same number of spaces.

Fig. 14

Tie on at 1A, pass around 1B, then 2A, 2B, 3A, 3B and so on until 11B is reached and tie off.

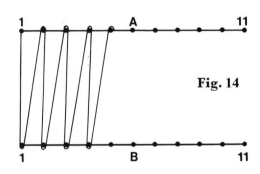

Fig. 14

Open method

Draw parallel lines and divide them into the same number of spaces.

Fig. 17

Tie on at 1A, pass around 1B, then 2A, 2B, 3A, 3B and so on until 21B.

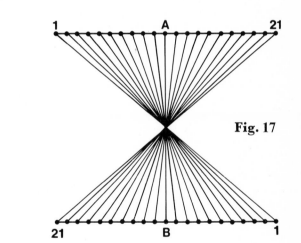

Fig. 17

Fig. 15, 16

The parallel lines can also be displaced as in example Fig. 15 or any distance apart even to the extent that the ends of the lines are displaced as in example Fig. 16. This example also shows that the lines could be different lengths as long as the number of dots are the same.

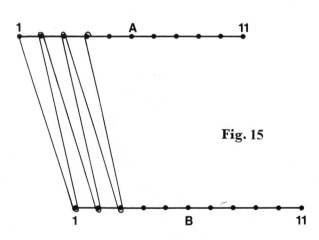

Fig. 15

Fig. 18

Shows the open method displaced.

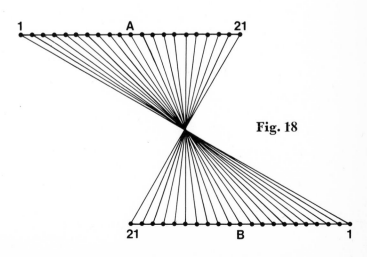

Fig. 18

Fig. 19
Shows the open method with one line half the length of the other.

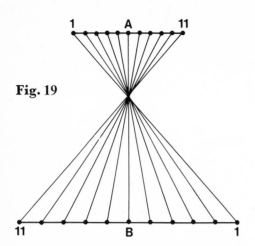

Fig. 19

Uses of parallel lines

A few of the designs later in the book have a heading, "Pattern additional information", this means that the principles used below apply.

1. On the 2.5cm (1in.) squared graph paper mark the Y axis to scale.
2. Mark the X axis to scale.
3. Draw the outline, only where it is not numbered.

Example Greek Galley.

4. On the X axis find the lowest point at which the outline reaches, on example 4cm (1.6in.).
5. Starting at the point 4cm (1.6in.) mark the axis every two small squares 5mm ($\frac{1}{5}$in.) apart until highest point of the outline is reached, on example 14cm (5.6in.).
6. Draw faint horizontal lines across the pattern, at each point on X axis.

i.e. 4cm (1.6in.), 4.5cm (1.8in.) 5cm (2in.) 5.2cm (2.2in.) etc, up to 14cm (5.6in.).

7. Where these horizontal lines strike the pattern outline mark a dot.

On example, line A has 4cm (1.6in.) to 12.6cm (5.2in.) equals 19 dots.

Line B has 6.5cm (2.6in.) to 12.6cm (5.2in.) equals 14 dots.

Line C has 4cm (1.6in.) to 14cm (5.6in.) equals 30 dots.

Line D has 6.5cm (2.6in.) to 12.6cm (5.2in.) equals 15 dots.

Line E has 4.5cm (1.8in.) to 7.5cm (3in.) equals 7 dots.

Line F has 4.5cm (1.8in.) to 6.5cm (2.6in.) equals 5 dots.

8. Now complete remainder of pattern.

9. The threading must be horizontal so only points on the same horizontal line can be joined together. To do this, tie on at 1A 4cm (1.6in.), pass to 1C 4cm (1.6in.).

Note Only those two points lie on the 4cm (1.6in.) horizontal line.

Then from 1C to 2A, in the normal way the next stage would be 2A to 2C, but on the same line is 1F, 1E, 10C and 11C, so we must thread 2A, to 1F, 1F to 3A, 3A to 2F, 2F to 4A and so on.

The spaces missed are filled in as follows.

Tie on again at 2C, pass to 10C, then 3C, 9C, 4C, 8C, 5c, 7C, 6C and tie off. The area from 2A to 10A is now completed. Tie on again at 1E, pass to 11C, then 2E, 12C, 3E, 13C, etc.

PATTERNS WITH THREE SIDED FIGURES
These are of two kinds:
1. Joined
2. Separate

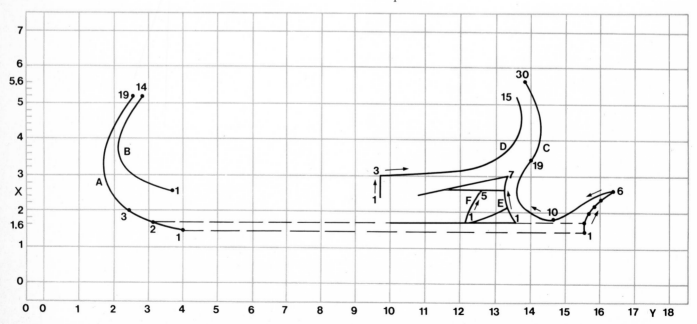

Joined

This means that all the sides are joined together, the example below will illustrate this.

Fig. 20

The pattern is made up as an equilateral triangle with the three sides of equal length and divided into the same number of spaces.

Tie on at 1A, around 1B, to 1C, then 2A, 2B, 2C, 3A, 3B, 3C and so on tying off at 11C.

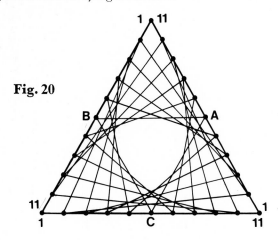

Fig. 20

You may have noticed that this shape is similar to that in Fig. 7. The reason is that part of Fig. 7 is a three sided figure which is made in exactly the same way.

From this it can be seen that all the patterns made with segments are three sided.

The three sides can be of different lengths and the angles could be all different, the important part is that all sides are divided into equal parts, even if all the sides are straight or curved.

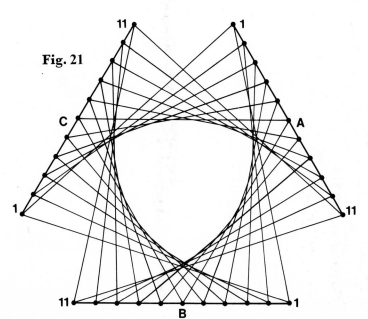

Fig. 21

Separate

This means that the sides are not joined together either in one corner or all corners.

Example Fig. 21 illustrates figure with none of the lines joined.

Fig. 21

Tie on at 1A, pass around 1B, to 1C, then 2A, 2B, 2C, 3A, 3B, 3C and so on tying off at 11C.

PATTERNS USING SQUARES, RECTANGLES AND PARALLELOGRAMS

The patterns and principles for squares, rectangles and parallelograms are exactly the same because each has four sides and the length of sides and the angles of the corners do not matter. The most important thing is that all sides are divided into the same number of spaces. Even if the sides are curved the principle is the same.

Fig. 22 (joined)

Tie on at 1D, pass around 1A, then 2D, 2A, 3D, 3A and so on until 21A, pass to 1C, then 2B, 2C, 3B, 3C and so on until 21C and tie off.

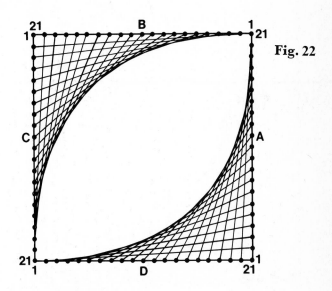

Fig. 22

Fig. 23 (joined)

Tie on at 1A, pass around 1B, 1C, 1D, then 2A, 2B, 2C, 2D and so on until 9D and tie off.

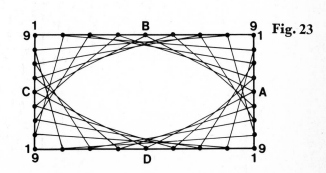

Fig. 23

Fig. 24 (separate)
Tie on at 1A, pass around 1B, 1C, 1D, then 2A, 2B, 2C, 2D and so on tying off at 6D.

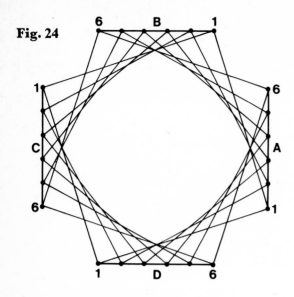

Fig. 24

on it. Place a set square across B-C and draw in the line BC. Place a ruler across the bottom edge of the set square and slide the set square parallel to line B-C until the next mark is in line with the edge of the set square, mark the line from AC to strike AB at 5. Repeat this procedure for all marks 1 to 4. The line AB will then be divided into the correct number of spaces required.

Method 3

When a line is curved place a piece of string or stiff wire along the outline then pull the string straight, mark the string or wire with the intervals required using either method 1 or method 2, place the string over the outline again and transfer the intervals from the string to the outline.

Method 4

For circles only
Divide 360° by the number of spaces required on the circle circumference, then using a protractor measure the angles out.

Example 1 $\dfrac{360°}{4} = 90° = 4$ spaces

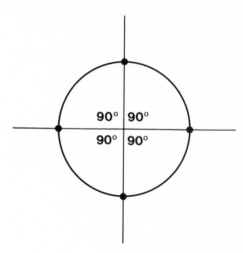

METHODS OF SPACING LINES

Method 1

Measure the straight line to be used and divide it by the number of intervals required, this will then give the space length required, so using a ruler mark the spaces out, or use a pair of compasses to strike out the space lengths.

Method 2

Draw a straight line of unknown length A-B, then at any angle around 30° to 40° draw a line of known length with the number of spaces required marked out

Example 2 $\dfrac{360°}{8} = 45° = 8$ spaces

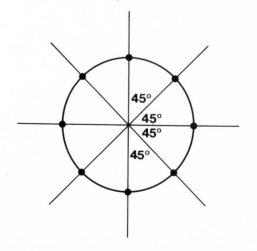

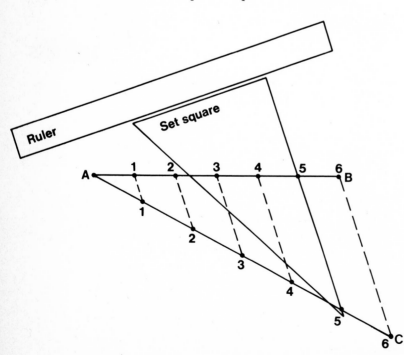

DESIGNING THE PATTERN

Straight line patterns

These patterns are very easy because when lines are straight they are easily divided into spaces.

The following example illustrates how easy they are to make.

Sketch the full size pattern to be used by using any of the basic patterns shown earlier, for this example a pattern made up of eight separate triangles (described in chapter on three sided figures) is used.

Draw the outline of the pattern and then decide the number of spaces required on each line but each line must have exactly the same number of spaces. A good guide is that on straight lines spaces should be around 5mm (1/5in.) to 1.25cm (1/2in.) in length.

Mark each separate triangle and number the pattern lines.

It can now be seen that each triangle when completed will be a similar shape to Fig. 21.

Note As the size of pattern required is made larger then more nails must be put in each line. The pattern for stargazer shows what the pattern will look like when completed but it is two thirds larger in size.

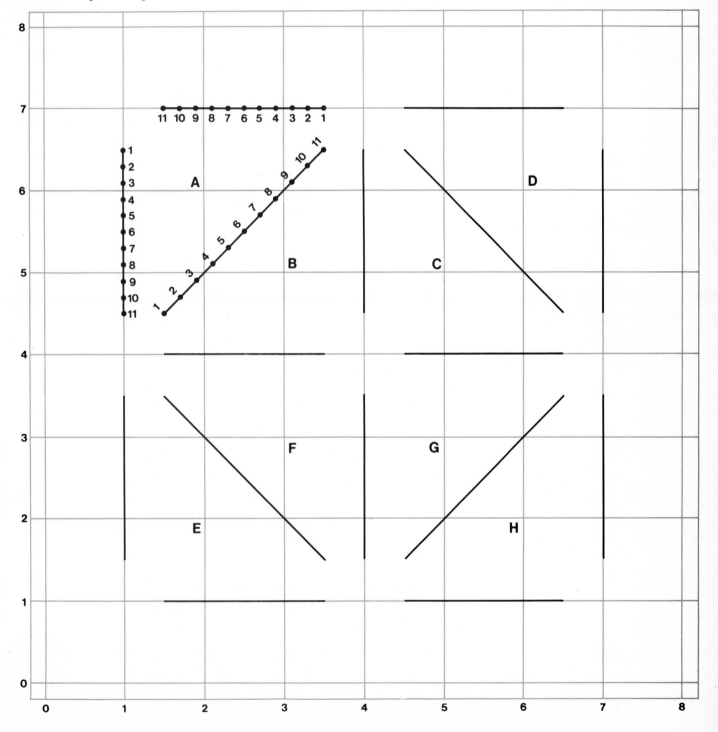

Curved line patterns

These are not quite as easy as straight line patterns but the same principles apply.

Select the picture to be used to make the pattern (in this case the Head of a Centurian).

Trace the outlines of the picture.

Transfer the outline of the picture onto 2.5mm (1/10in.) squared graph paper as shown in Fig. A.

The size of picture required can then be decided by multiplying the 2.5mm (1/10in.) scale by the scale required. In this example 2.5mm (1/10in.) × 5 equals 1.25cm (1/2in.) per square. Then using 2.5cm (1in.) squared graph paper the pattern outline can be plotted by using intersecting points on the X and Y axis.

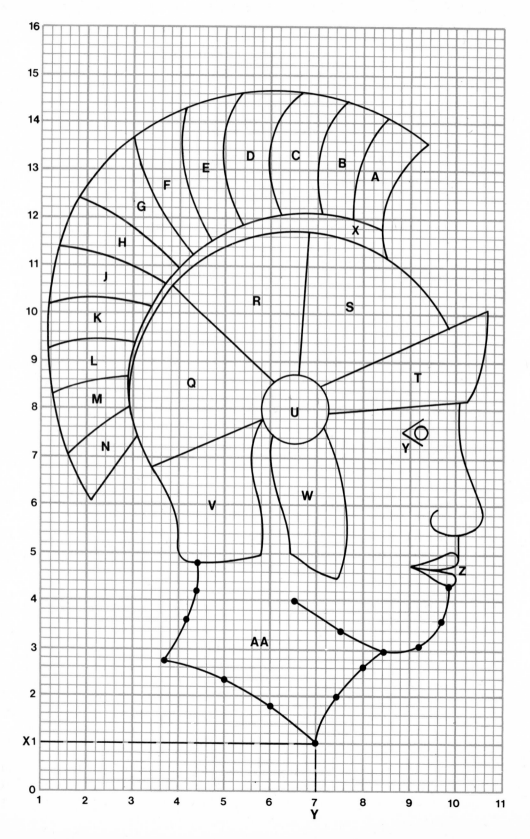

Plotting the neck

X	1	3	2.75	4	4.4	5	2	1.8	2.3	3.4	3	3.6	3.6	4.2
Y	9	10.5	5.75	8.5	11.8	12	9.4	8	7	9.4	11.2	11.7	6.2	6.4

The rest of the pattern is plotted in the same way, then when these points have been plotted join the dots together. If more plotted points are required follow the same principle.

At this stage the outline is completed and the design to be used has to be decided using the basic patterns shown earlier in the book.

The suggested patterns for this design are:

1. Patterns A to N and W are basically rectangles with curved sides, so all four sides have same number of nails.
2. Pattern U is a circle and can be treated as a fill in type.
3. Q to S and V are basically joined triangles and must have the same number of nails in all three sides.
4. T is basically a separate triangle and must have the same number of nails in all three sides.
5. Y is an angle of less than 90° and both sides must have the same number of nails.
6. The eye is just an elipse and can be treated as a fill in type circle.
7. X is basically two parallel lines and can be treated as a fill-in type.
8. Z is two elongated elipses coming to a point at one end and can be treated as a fill in type circle.

The pattern can be seen completed in centurian pattern later in the book.

MAKING THE PICTURE
You will need:

Wood 1.25cm (1/2in) chipboard is most suitable because it is light in weight but almost any scrap pieces of board could be used.

Covering fabric Velvet is the most suitable fabric because of its beautiful finish but felt or hessian could be used. You could also just paint the board in a pleasing background colour.

Nails 1.5cm (3/4in.) panel pins with a good head on them to stop cotton pulling off.

Galvanised nails are preferable because they will not tarnish. Where silvery thread is used use silver nails but where golden coloured thread is used use brass or copper coloured nails, this will prevent any clash in the pattern. 1.5cm (3/4in.) tacks are used for fastening the velvet to the board.

Thread Lurex thread gives a bright shiny effect but any good quality thread would be suitable.

Beading 1.5cm (5/8in.) beading for border, D-shape easiest to put on, nail on with 1.5cm (3/4in.) moulding pins.

Graph paper 2.5cm (1in.) squares. For every pattern, draw an actual size plan on the paper, using a dot to represent each nail. These dots should be spaced evenly along each line.

Stages of assembly

1. Saw the board to size making sure that all corners are 90°.
2. Nail fabric along the longest side of the board making sure that the fabric is taut, this stops material wrinkling. The nails must be spaced no more than 5cm (2in.) apart otherwise the fabric bows when taut.

The next side to be nailed is the one opposite the side just nailed, keep material taut.

Next nail the other two sides making sure that any wrinkles in the material are eliminated.

3. Place the pattern over the board and put nails in each corner to hold the pattern square and steady. Nail through dots on pattern working from the centre to the outside. When all nails are in pull pattern over the heads of the nails to remove it.

To ensure that all the nails are at the same height put a pencil at the side of the nail head and hammer the nail until level with the pencil.

4. Tying on and tying off are very basic procedures. The best type of knot for string pictures is the clove hitch, this is made by making two half hitches over the nail. This knot lies flat against the nail and will not look bulky, the tighter the thread is pulled the tighter the knot will become.

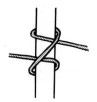

Clove Hitch   **Half Hitch**

When pattern is completed cut all excess thread ends off and put a spot of glue on the knot as an extra measure to stop thread moving.

5. Cut beading lengths to exact length of sides of board with mitred edges of 45° to give a good joint at the corners, nail at about 15cm (6in.) intervals.

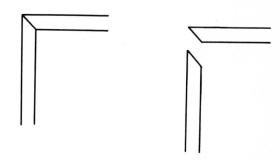

6. Trim off excess velvet at back of picture and cover rough edge with masking tape to prevent frayed edges.
7. If the corners are rough file them square and fill any gaps with plastic wood.

PICTURE
COLLECTION

Instructions on page 21

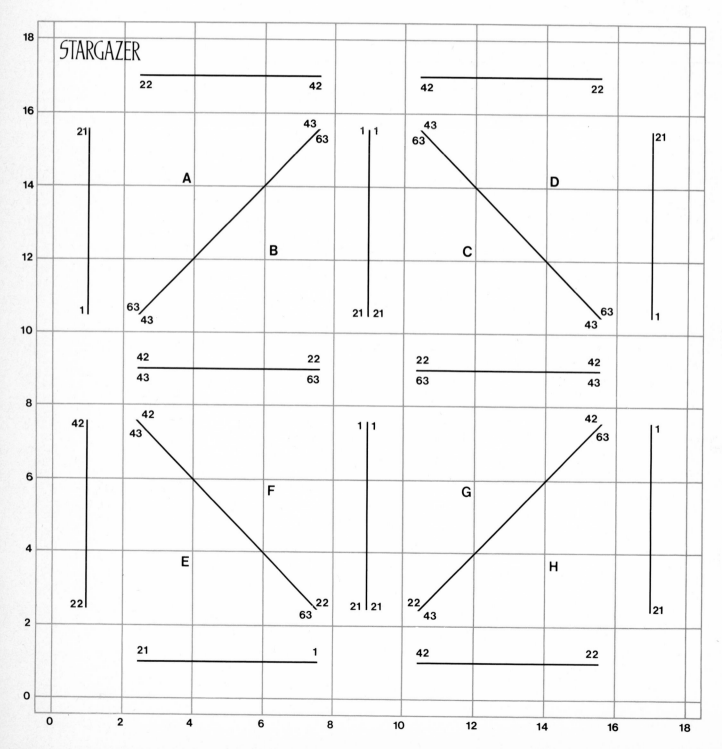

STARGAZER

STARGAZER

You will need

Chipboard 45cm (18in) × 45cm (18in), velvet 50cm (20in) × 50cm (20in), 336 panel pins, silver and blue thread and one sheet of 2.5cm (1in) squared graph paper.

Threading the pattern

Triangle A

Tie on with blue at 1A, pass to 22A, then 43A, 2A, 23A, 44A, 3A, 24A, 45A, 4A, 25A, 46A, 5A, 26A, 47A, 6A, 27A, 48A, 7A, 28A, 49A and so on in this sequence until 63A and tie off.

Triangle B

Tie on with silver at 1B, pass to 22B, then 43B, 2B, 23B, 44B, 3B, 24B, 45B, 4B, 25B, 46B, 5B, 26B, 47B, 6B, 27B, 48B, 7B, 28B, 49B and so on in this sequence until 63B and tie off.

Triangle C

Tie on with blue at 1C, pass to 22C, then 43C, 2C, 23C, 44C, 3C, 24C, 45C, 4C, 25C, 46C, 5C, 26C, 47C, 6C, 27C, 48C, 7C, 28C, 49C and so on in this sequence until 63C and tie off.

Triangle D

Tie on with silver at 1D, pass to 22D, then 43D, 2D, 23D, 44D, 3D, 24D, 45D, 4D, 25D, 46D, 5D, 26D, 47D, 6D, 27D, 48D, 7D, 28D, 49D and so on in this sequence until 63D and tie off.

Triangle E

Tie on with silver at 1E, pass to 22E, then 43E, 2E, 23E, 44E, 3E, 24E, 45E, 4E, 25E, 46E, 5E, 26E, 47E, 6E, 27E, 48E, 7E, 28E, 49E and so on in this sequence until 63E and tie off.

Triangle F

Tie on with blue at 1F, pass to 22F, then 43F, 2F, 23F, 44F, 3F, 24F, 45F, 4F, 25F, 46F, 5F, 26F, 47F, 6F, 27F, 48F, 7F, 28F, 49F and so on in this sequence until 63F and tie off.

Triangle G

Tie on with silver at 1G, pass to 22G, then 43G, 2G, 23G, 44G, 3G, 24G, 45G, 4G, 25G, 46G, 5G, 26G, 47G, 6G, 27G, 48G, 7G, 28G, 49G and so on in this sequence until 63G and tie off.

Triangle H

Tie on with blue at 1H, pass to 22H, then 43H, 2H, 23H, 44H, 3H, 24H, 45H, 4H, 25H, 46H, 5H, 26H, 47H, 6H, 27H, 48H, 7H, 28H, 49H and so on in this sequence until 63H and tie off.

SPINNER

You will need

Chipboard 35cm (14in) × 35cm (14in), velvet 40cm (16in) × 40cm (16in), 108 panel pins, gold and green thread and one sheet of 2.5cm (1in) squared graph paper.

Threading the pattern

Tie on with gold at 1A, pass to 1H, then 2A, 2H, 3A, 3H, 4A, 4H, 5A, 5H, 6A, 6H, 7A, 7H, 8A, 8H, 9A, 9H and tie off.

Tie on with gold at 1B, pass to 1J, then 2B, 2J, 3B, 3J, 4B, 4J, 5B, 5J, 6B, 6J, 7B, 7J, 8B, 8J, 9B, 9J and tie off.

Tie on with gold at 1C, pass to 1K, then 2C, 2K, 3C, 3K, 4C, 4K, 5C, 5K, 6C, 6K, 7C, 7K, 8C, 8K, 9C, 9K and tie off.

Tie on with gold at 1D, pass to 1L, then 2D, 2L, 3D, 3L, 4D, 4L, 5D, 5L, 6D, 6L 7D, 7L, 8D, 8L, 9D, 9L and tie off.

Tie on with gold at 1E, pass to 1M, then 2E, 2M, 3E, 3M, 4E, 4M, 5E, 5M, 6E, 6M, 7E, 7M, 8E, 8M, 9E, 9M and tie off.

Tie on with gold at 1F, pass to 1G, then 2F, 2G, 3F, 3G, 4F, 4G, 5F, 5G, 6F, 6G, 7F, 7G, 8F, 8G, 9F, 9G and tie off.

Tie on with green at 1A, pass to 1M, then 2A, 2M, 3A, 3M, 4A, 4M, 5A, 5M, 6A, 6M, 7A, 7M, 8A, 8M, 9A, 9M and tie off.

Tie on with green at 1B, pass to 1G, then 2B, 2G, 3B, 3G, 4B, 4G, 5B, 5G, 6B, 6G, 7B, 7G, 8B, 8G, 9B, 9G and tie off.

Tie on with green at 1C, pass to 1H, then 2C, 2H, 3C, 3H, 4C, 4H, 5C, 5H, 6C, 6H, 7C, 7H, 8C, 8H, 9C, 9H and tie off.

Tie on with green at 1D, pass to 1J, then 2D, 2J, 3D, 3J, 4D, 4J, 5D, 5J, 6D, 6J, 7D, 7J, 8D, 8J, 9D, 9J and tie off.

Tie on with green at 1E, pass to 1K, then 2E, 2K, 3E, 3K, 4E, 4K, 5E, 5K, 6E, 6K, 7E, 7K, 8E, 8K, 9E, 9K and tie off.

Tie on with green at 1F, pass to 1L, then 2F, 2L, 3F, 3L, 4F, 4L, 5F, 5L, 6F, 6L, 7F, 7L, 8F, 8L, 9F, 9L and tie off.

Diagram on page 22

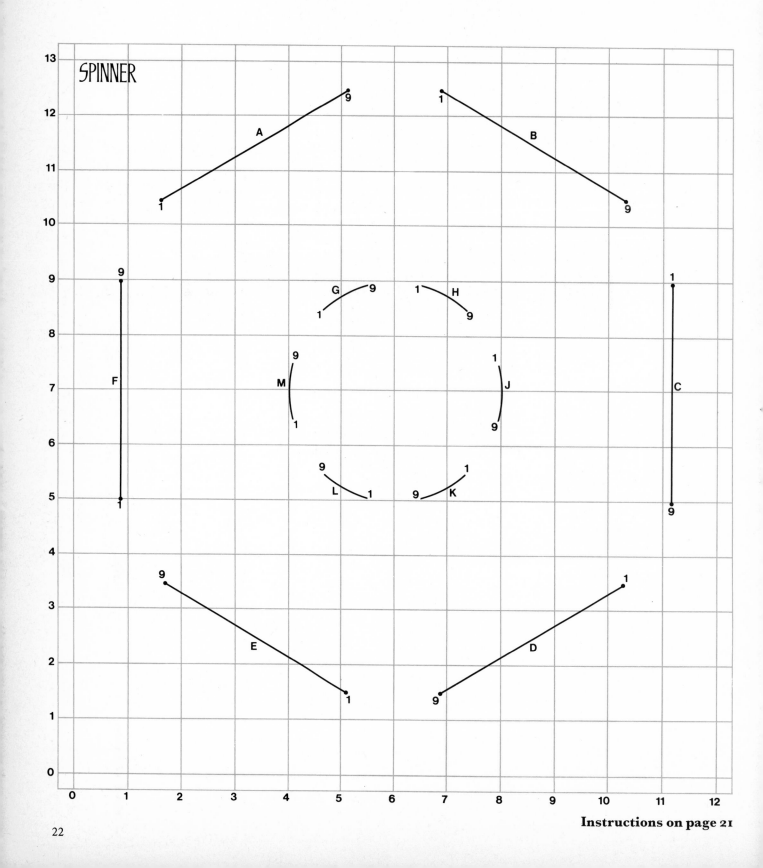

SPINNER

Instructions on page 21

24

WINDMILL

You will need
Chipboard 37.5cm (15in) × 22.5cm (9in), velvet 42.5cm (17in) × 27.5cm (11in), 300 panel pins, brown, turquoise, orange, lime green and red thread and one sheet of 2.5cm (1in) squared graph paper.

Threading the pattern
Body (A)
Tie on with brown at 1A, pass to 34A, then 2A, 33A, 3A, 32A, 4A, 31A, 5A, 30A, 6A, 29A, 7A, 28A, 8A, 27A, 9A, 26A, 10A, 25A and so on in this sequence until 17A and tie off.

Roof (B)
Tie on with turquoise at 1B, then pass to 2B, then 1B, 3B, 1B, 4B, 1B, 5B, 1B, 6B, 1B, 7B, 1B, 8B, 1B, 9B and so on in this sequence until 24B and tie off.

Vane (C)
Tie on with orange at X, pass to 1C, then X, 2C, X, 3C, X, 4C, X, 5C, X, 6C, X, 7C and so on in this sequence until 28C and tie off.

Door (J)
Tie on with red at 1J, pass to 12J, then 2J, 11J, 3J, 10J, 4J, 9J, 5J, 8J, 6J, 7J and tie off.

Steps (K)
Tie on with brown at 1K, pass to 8K, then 7K, 2K, 3K, 6K, 5K, 4K, 3K, 6K, 7K, 2K, 1K and tie off.

Vane support (Y)
Tie on with brown at 1Y, pass to 2Y, then 13Y, 12Y, 2Y, 3Y, 10Y, 11Y, 3Y, 4Y, 5Y, 6Y, 7Y, 8Y, 9Y and tie off.

Arm (G)
Tie on with lime at Z, pass to 33G, then 1G, 32G, 2G, 31G, 3G, 30G, 4G, 29G, 5G, 28G, 6G, 27G, 7G, 26G, 8G, 25G, 9G, 24G, 10G and so on in this sequence until 18G, then 17G, Z and tie off.
Tie on with orange at Z, pass to 18G, then Z, 17G, Z and tie off.

Arm (F)
Tie on with lime at Z, pass to 29F, then 1F, 28F, 2F, 27F, 3F and so on in this sequence until 16F, then 15F, Z and tie off.
Tie on with orange at Z, pass to 16F, then Z, 15F, Z and tie off.

Arm (E)
Tie on with lime at Z, pass to 46E, then 1E, 45E, 2E, 44E, 3E, 43E, 4E, 42E, 5E, 41E, 6E, 40E and so on in this sequence until 24E, then 23E, Z and tie off.
Tie on with orange at Z, pass to 24E, Z, 23E, Z and tie off.

Arm (D)
Tie on with lime at Z, pass to 30D, then 1D, 29D, 2D, 28D, 3D, 27D, 4D, 26D, 5D, 25D, 6D, 24D and so on in this sequence until 16D, then 15D, Z and tie off.
Tie on with orange at Z, pass to 16D, then Z, 15D, Z and tie off.

Arm (H)
Tie on with lime at Z, pass to 42H, then 1H, 41H, 2H, 40H, 3H, 39H, 4H, 38H. 5H, 37H, 6H, 36H, 7H, 35H, 8H, 34H and so on in this sequence until 22H, then 21H, Z and tie off.
Tie on with orange at Z, pass to 22H, Z, 21H, Z and tie off.

Diagram on page 26

WINDMILL

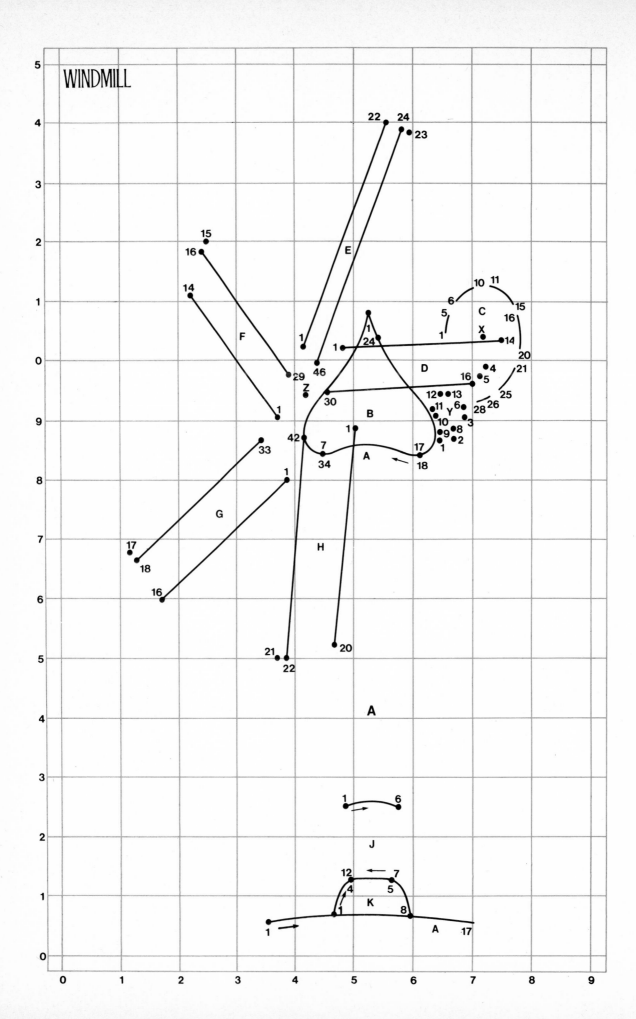

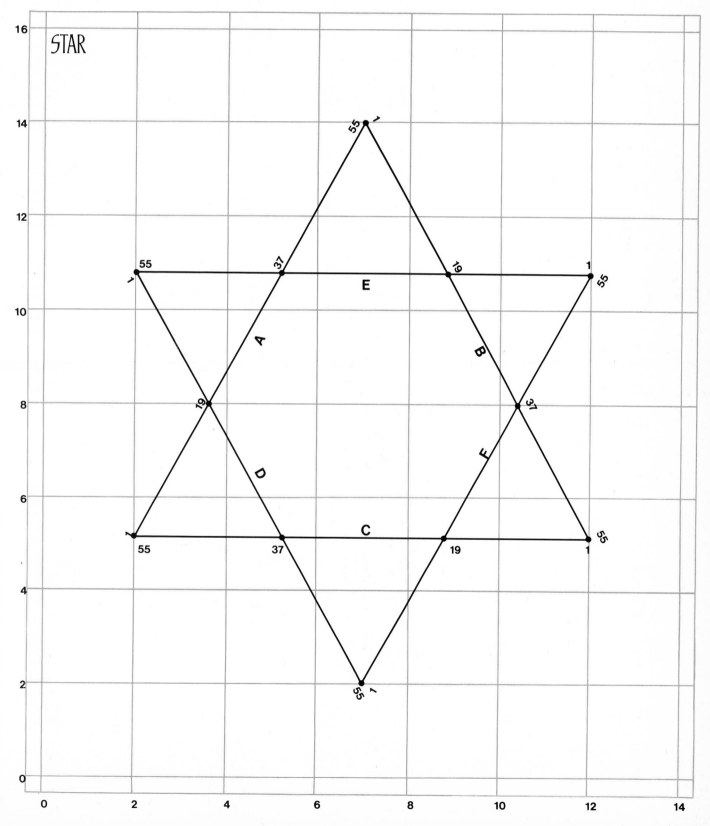

STAR

STAR

You will need
Chipboard 40cm (16in) × 35cm (14in), velvet 45cm (18in) × 40cm (16in), 318 panel pins, green and gold thread and one sheet of 2.5cm (1in) squared graph paper.

Threading the pattern
Tie on with green at 1A, pass to 1B, then 1C, 2A, 2B, 2C, 3A, 3B, 3C, 4A, 4B, 4C and so on in this sequence until 55C and tie off.

Tie on with gold at 1D, pass to 1E, then 1F, 2D, 2E, 2F, 3D, 3E, 3F, 4D, 4E, 4F and so on in this sequence until 55F and tie off.

Tie on with green at 1A, pass to 19D, then 37C, 2A, 20D, 38C, 3A, 21D, 39C, 4A, 22D, 40C and so on in this sequence until 55C and tie off.

Tie on with green at 1C, pass to 19F, then 37B, 2C, 20F, 38B, 3C, 21F, 39B, 4C, 22F, 40B and so on in this sequence until 55B and tie off.

Tie on with green at 1B, pass to 19E, then 37A, 2B, 20E, 38A, 3B, 21E, 39A, 4B, 22E, 40A and so on in this sequence until 55A and tie off.

Diagram on page 27

GREEK GALLEY

You will need
Chipboard 45cm (18in) × 27.5cm (11in), velvet 50cm (20in) × 32.5cm (13in), 410 panel pins, brown, blue, red, turquoise, silver, gold and orange thread and one sheet of 2.5cm (1in) squared graph paper.

Pattern additional information
Draw the outline D, then starting from the base of the galley mark horizontal lines across the outline every 1½ squares 3.75mm (3/20in) vertically. (See chapter on parallel lines).

Threading the pattern
Thread galley outline as for parallel area using brown.

Eye (X & W)
Tie on with turquoise at 1W, pass to 5W, then 2W, 6W, 3W, 7W, 4W, 8W, 5W, 1W again and tie off.
Tie on with silver at 1X, pass to 2X, then 3X, 4X, 5X, 6X, 2X, 7X, 2X, 8X, 2X and tie off. Tie on at 23X, pass to 16X, then 15X, 16X, 14X, 16X, pass from 16X, to 22X on outside of the nails and tie off.

Shelter (F)
Tie on with turquoise at 7F, pass to 8F, then on inside of 8F, 9F, 10F, 11F, 12F, 13F, 14F, then on outside back to 8F, then 15F, 6F, 16F, 5F, 17F, 4F, 18F, 3F and so on in this sequence until 26F and tie off.

Shield (T)
Tie on with red at 1T, pass to 7T, then 2T, 8T, 3T, 9T, 4T, 10T, 5T, 11T, 6T, 12T, 7T, 1T and tie off.
Repeat for Shields G, H, J, K, L, M, N, P, Q, R, S, Y and C.
Note Shields red/blue Alternate.

Oars (T)
Tie on with orange at 5T, pass to 1U, then 24U, then 1U and tie off.

Oars (S)
Tie on with orange at 5S, pass to 2U, then 23U, then 2U and tie off.

Oars (R)
Tie on with orange at 5R, pass to 3U, then 22U, then 3U and tie off.
Repeat for oars G, H, J, K, L, M, N, P and Q, using same method.

Mast (Z)
Tie on with orange at 15A, pass to 1Z, then 2Z, 1Z, 32A and tie off.
Tie on at 3Z, pass to 4Z (also 1R), then back to 3Z and tie off.

Sail (A)
Tie on with gold at 43A, pass to 44A, 43A, 45A, 43A, 46A, 43A, 47A, 43A, 48A, 43A, 1A, 43A, 2A, 43A, 3A, 43A, 4A, 43A, 5A and so on in this sequence until 42A and tie off.

Rear (E)
Tie on with gold at 1E, pass to 9E, then 17E, 2E, 10E, 18E, 3E, 11E, 19E, 4E, 12E, 20E, 5E, 13E, 21E, 6E, 14E, 22E, 7E, 15E, 23E, 8E, 16E, 24E and tie off.

Fluting (B)
Tie on with brown at 1C, pass to 1B, then 1C, 2B, 1C, 3B, 1C, pass to 3C, then 5B, 3C, 6B, 3C, 7B, 3C and tie off.
Tie on with silver at 2C, pass to 3B, then 2C, 4B, 2C, 5B, pass to 4C, then 7B, 4C, 8B, 4C, 9B, 4C and tie off.

Section (C)
Tie on with brown at 1C, pass to 7C, then 2C, 8C, 3C, 9C, 4C, 10C, 5C, 11C, 6C, 12C, 7C, 1C and tie off.
Repeat for Section Y.

Diagram on page 30–31

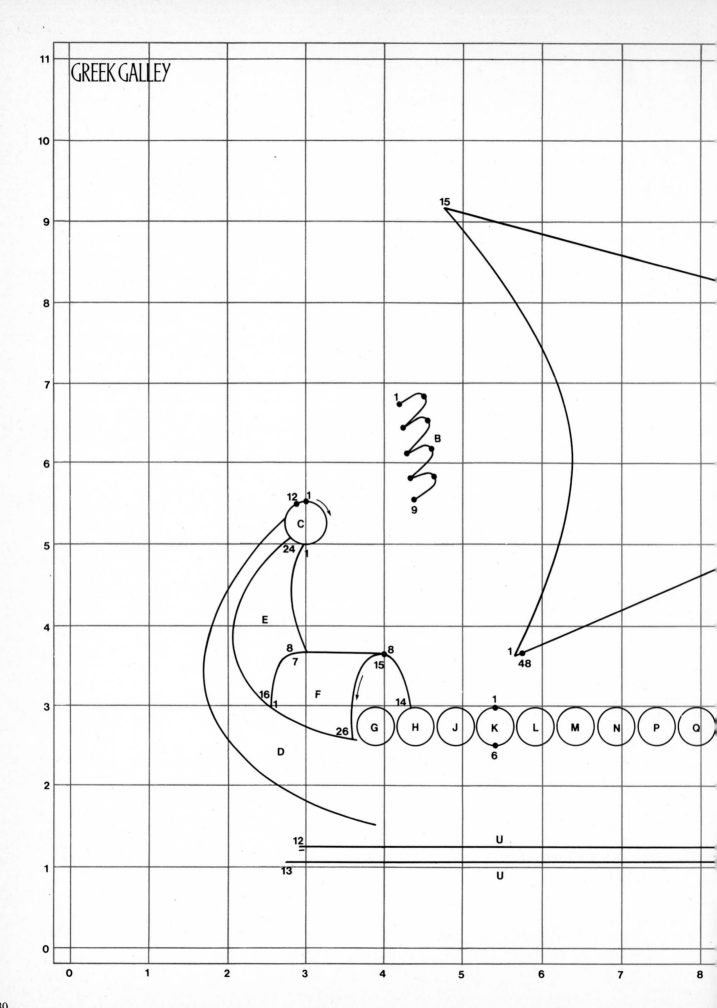

GREEK GALLEY

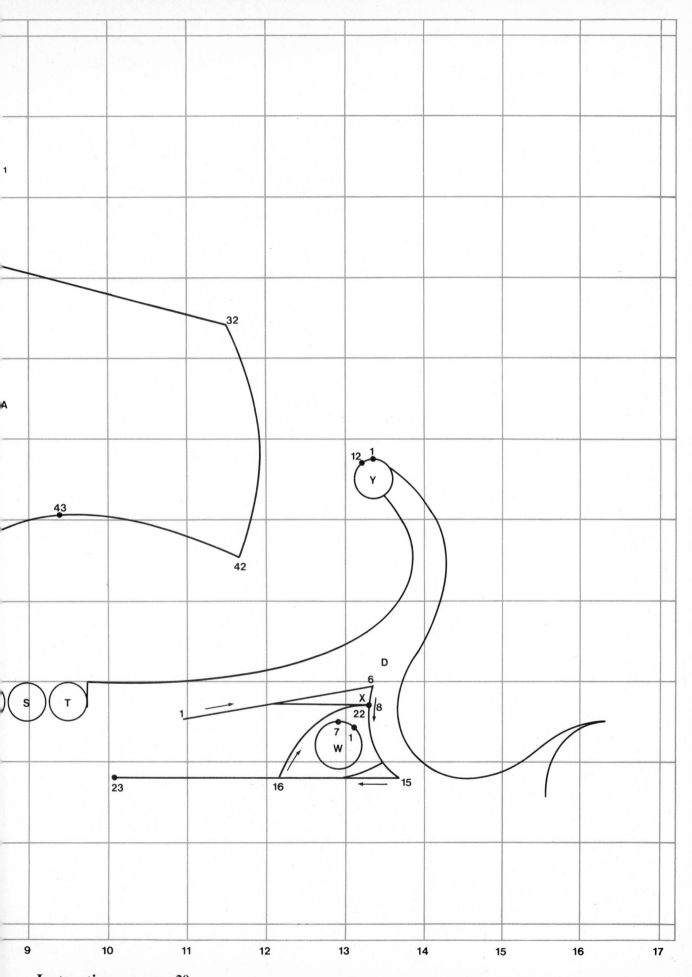

Instructions on page 29

HORSE & CART

You will need
Chipboard 47.5cm (19in) × 22.5cm (9in), velvet 52.5cm (21in) × 27.5cm (11in), 300 panel pins, brown, gold, orange, green, silver and turquoise thread and one sheet of 2.5cm (1in) squared graph paper.

Pattern additional information
Draw the outline of the horse only, then starting at the base of the horse mark horizontal lines at intervals of 1½ squares 3.75mm (3/20in). Across the outline where the horizontal lines strike the outline put a dot. (See chapter on parallel lines).

Threading the pattern
Thread horse outline as for parallel area using brown, then tie on at 11ZZ, pass to 10ZZ, 9ZZ, 8ZZ, 7ZZ, 6ZZ, 5ZZ, 4ZZ, 3ZZ, 2ZZ, 1ZZ, then 5M, 6M, 7M, 8M and so on right around the edge of the horse, then use same system to fill in horse's leg lines and leg muscle lines.

Cart (A)
Tie on with gold at 1A, pass to 10A, then 2A, 9A, 3A, 8A, 4A, 7A, 5A, 6A and tie off.
Tie on with orange at 18C, pass to 5B, then 17C, 6B, 16C, 7B, 15C, 8B, 14C, 9B, 13C, 10B, 12C, 11B, 11C, 12B, 10C, 13B, 9C, 14B, 8C, 15B, 7C, 24D, 6C, 25D, 5C and tie off.
Tie on with gold at 1C, pass to 22C, then 2C, 21C, 3C, 20C, 4C, 19C and tie off. Tie on at 8C, pass to 15B, then 9C, 14B, 9C, 14B, 8C, 15B, pass to 5B, then 16B, 4B, 17B, 3B, 18B, 2B, 19B, 1B and tie off.
Tie on at 1X, pass to 1Z, then 2X, 2Z, 3X, 3Z, 4X, 4Z and tie off.
Tie on at 1Y, pass to 1W, then 2Y, 2W, 3Y, 3W, 4Y, 4W and tie off.

Continued over

HORSE & CART

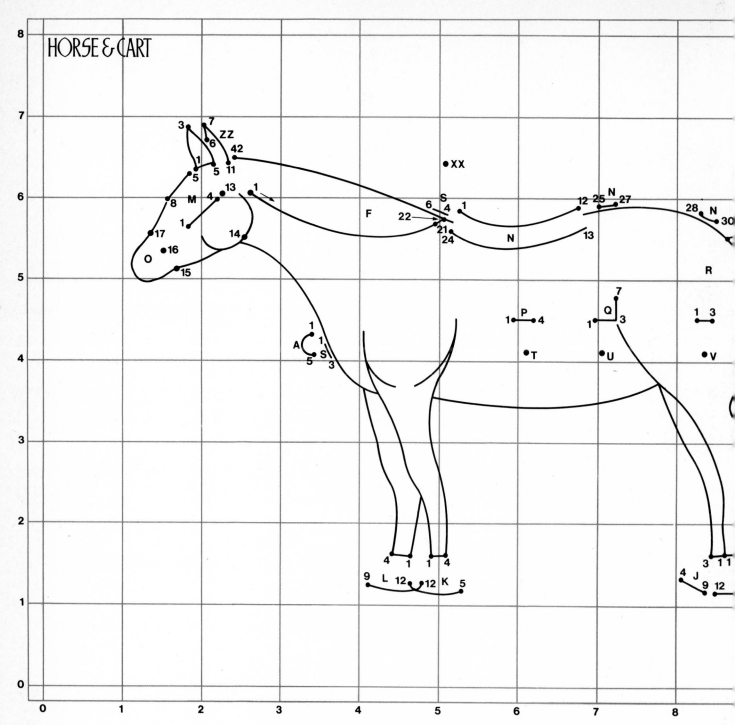

Load (D)

Tie on with green at 9D, pass to 8D, then 10D, 7D, 11D, 6D, 12D, 5D, 13D, 4D, 14D, 3D, 15D, 2D, 16D, 1D, 17D, 26D, 18D, 25D, 19D, 24D, 20D, 23D, 21D, 22D and tie off.

Wheel (E)

Tie on with brown at 1E, pass to 9E, then 2E, 10E, 3E, 11E, 4E, 12E, 5E, 13E, 6E, 14E, 7E, 15E, 8E, 16E, 9E, 17E, 10E, 18E, 11E, 19E and so on in this sequence until 1E again and tie off. Tie on at 73E, pass to 81E, then 74E, 82E, 75E, 83E, 76E, 84E, 77E, 85E, 78E, 86E, 79E, 87E and so on in this sequence until 73E again, then pass to 37E, 73E, 38E, 73E, 39E, 73E, then 75E, 40E, 75E, 41E, 75E, 42E, 75E, then 77E, 43E, 77E, 44E, 77E, 45E, 77E, then 79E and so on in this sequence until 73E again and tie off.

Tie on with gold at 97E, pass to 102E, then 98E, 103E, 99E, 104E, 100E, 105E, 101E, 106E, 102E, 97E and tie off.

Horse's mane (F)

Tie on with silver at 1F, pass to 42F, then 2F, 41F, 3F, 40F, 4F, 39F, 5F, 38F, 6F, 37F, 7F, 36F, 8F, 35F, 9F, 34F, 10F and so on in this sequence until 22F and tie off.

Tail (G)

Tie on with silver at 1G, pass to 22G, then 2G, 21G, 3G, 20G, 4G, 19G, 5G, 18G, 6G, 17G, 7G, 16G, 8G, 15G, 9G, 14G, 10G and so on in this sequence until 11G and tie off..

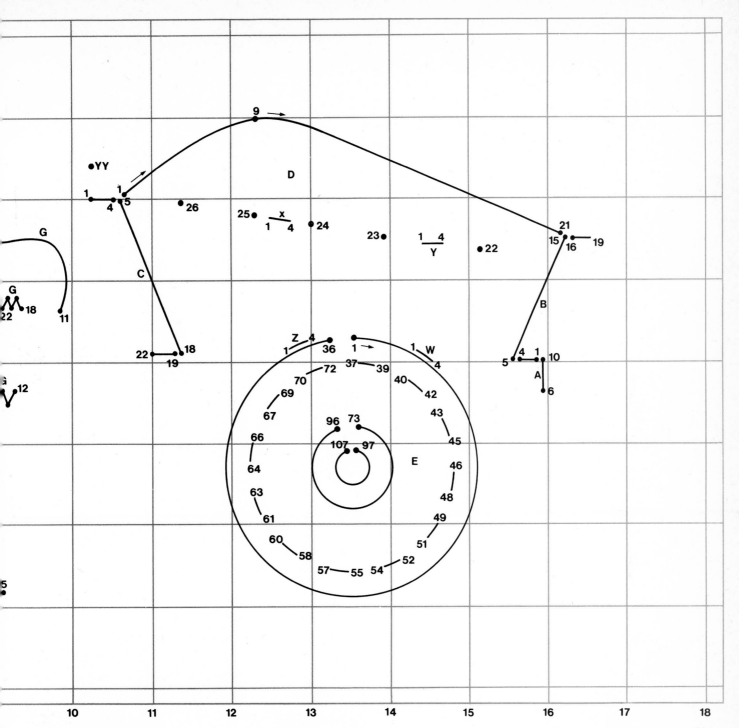

Feet (H, K, L & J)
Tie on with silver at 4H, pass to 5H, then 4H, 6H, 3H, 7H, 3H, 8H, 2H, 9H, 2H, 10H, 1H, 11H, 1H, 12H and tie off.
Repeat for Feet K and L.
Tie on with silver at 1J, pass to 9J, then 1J, 8J, 2J, 7J, 2J, 6J, 3J, 5J, 3J, 4J and tie off.

Blinker (M)
Tie on with turquoise at 1M, pass to 8M, then 2M, 7M, 3M, 6M, 4M, 5M and tie off.

Hitching gear
Tie on with turquoise at 1N, pass to 24N, then 2N, 23N, 3N, 22N, 4N, 21N and so on in this sequence until 13N, pass to 5N, then 1P, 5N, 2P, 6N, 3P, 6N, 4P, pass to T, then 4P and tie off. Tie on at 1Q, pass to 25N, then 2Q, 26N, 3Q, 27N, 4Q, pass to U, then 4Q, from 4Q, pass to 34N, then 5Q, 33N, 6Q, 32N, 7Q, 31N and tie off.
Tie on at 1R, pass to 28N, 2R, 29N, 3R, 30N, 3R, pass to V, then 3R and tie off.

Tie on at 1S, pass to 6S, then 2S, 5S, 3S, 4S and tie off.

Harness (M)
Tie on with turquoise at 4M, pass to 14M, then 13M, 16M, 15M, 17M, 16M and tie off.

Reins
Tie on with turquoise at 15M, pass to XX, then 22F, XX, YY, 3C, YY, 3D, and tie off.

37

38

GALLEON

You will need
Chipboard 60cm (24in) × 40cm (16in), velvet 65cm (26in) × 45cm (18in), 720 panel pins, red and silver thread and one sheet of 2.5cm (1in) squared graph paper.

Threading the pattern
Main sail (K)
Tie on with silver at Pin MM, pass to 1K, then Pin MM, 2K, Pin MM, 3K, Pin MM, 4K, Pin MM, 5K, Pin MM, 6K, Pin MM, 7K, Pin MM, 8K, and so on in this sequence until 55K and tie off.
Sail (A) is the same as sail (K) so repeat the procedure using Pin LL for centre.

Main sail (J)
Tie on with silver at Pin P, pass to 1J, then Pin P, 2J, Pin P, 3J, Pin P, 4J, Pin P, 5J, Pin P, 6J, Pin P, 7J, Pin P, 8J and so on in this sequence until 51J and tie off.
Sail (B) is the same as Sail (J) so repeat the procedure using Pin N for centre.

Main sail (H)
Tie on with silver at Pin R, pass to 1H, then Pin R, 2H, Pin R, 3H, Pin R, 4H, Pin R, 5H, Pin R, 6H, Pin R, 7H, Pin R, 8H, Pin R, 9H and so on in this sequence until 48H and tie off.
Sail (C) is the same as Sail (H) so repeat the procedure using Pin Q for centre.

Main sail (G)
Tie on with silver at Pin T, pass to 1G, then Pin T, 2G, Pin T, 3G, Pin T, 4G, Pin T, 5G, Pin T, 6G, Pin T, 7G, Pin T, 8G and so on in this sequence until 49G and tie off.
Sail (D) is the same as sail (G) so repeat the procedure using Pin S for centre.

Main sail (F)
Tie on with silver at Pin V, pass to 1F, then Pin V, 2F, Pin V, 3F, Pin V, 4F, Pin V, 5F, Pin V, 6F, Pin V, 7F, Pin V, 8F and so on in this sequence until 35F and tie off.
Sail (E) is the same as Sail (F) so repeat the procedure using Pin U for centre.

Rigging
Tie on with silver at 10F, pass over Pin XX to 26F and tie off.
Tie on at 10E, pass over Pin WW to 26E and tie off.

Front sail (W)
Tie on with silver at 1W, pass to 20W, then 2W, 21W, 3W, 22W, 4W, 23W, 5W, 24W, 6W, 25W, 7W, 8W and so on in this sequence until 39W, then pass to 40W, 41W, 20W and tie off.

Front sail (Y)
Tie on with silver at 1Y, pass to 20Y, then 2Y, 21Y, 3Y, 22Y, 4Y, 23Y, 5Y, 24Y, 6Y, 25Y, 7Y, 26Y, 8Y and so on in this sequence until 39Y, then pass to 40Y, 41Y, 20Y and tie off.

Front sail (Z)
Tie on with silver at 1Z, pass to 20Z, then 2Z, 21Z, 3Z, 22Z, 4Z, 23Z, 5Z, 24Z, 6Z, 25Z, 7Z, 26Z, 8Z and so on in this sequence until 39Z, then pass to 40Z, 41Z, 20Z and tie off.

Front sail (X)
Tie on with silver at 1X, pass to 20X, then 2X, 21X, 3X, 22X, 4X, 23X, 5X, 24X, 6X, 25X, 7X, 26X, 8X and so on in this sequence until 39X, then pass to 40X, 41X, 42X, 20X and tie off.

Side (L)
Tie on with red at 1L, pass to 45L, then 2L, 44L, 3L, 43L, 4L, 42L, 5L, 41L, 6L, 40L, 7L, 39L, 8L, then pass to 33L, then 45L, 31L, 44L, 29L, 43L, 27L, 42L, 25L, 41L, 23L, 40L, 21L and so on in this sequence until 8L and tie off.

Side (M)
Tie on with red at 1M, pass to 45L, then 2M, 44L, 3M, 43L, 4M, 42L, 5M, 41L, 6M, 40L and so on in this sequence until 33L, then pass to 45L, then 33L, 44L, 16M, 43L, 15M, 42L, 14M, 41L, 13M, 40L, 12M, 39L, 11M, 38L and tie off.

Front arm
Tie on with red at Pin XY, pass to 34L, then XY, 33L, XY, 32L, XY, 31L and tie off.

Diagram on page 40

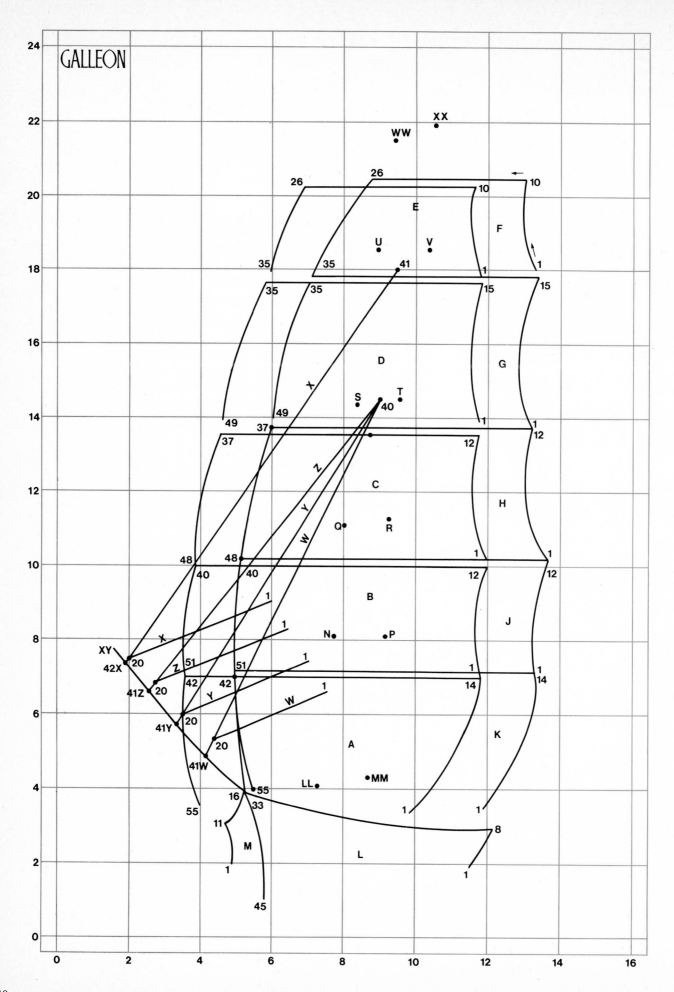

GALLEON

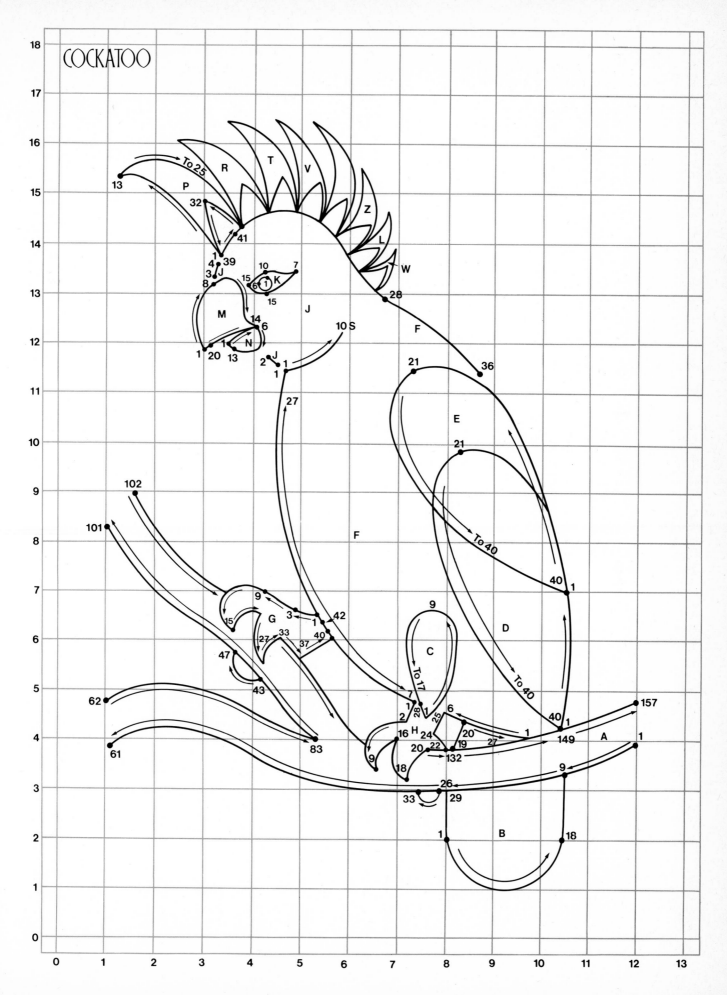

COCKATOO

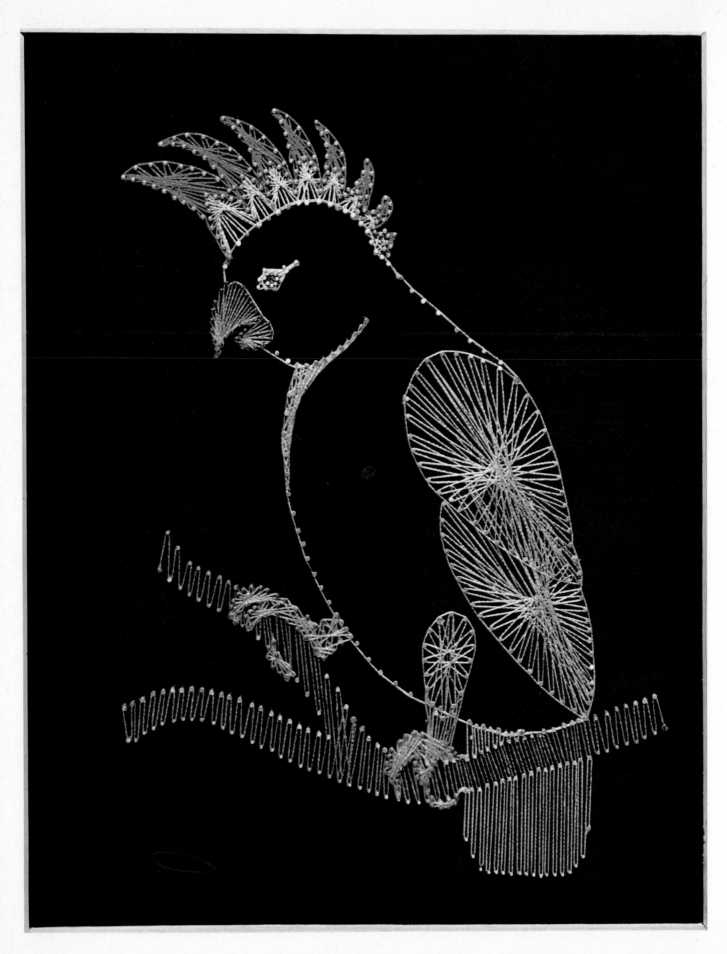

42

COCKATOO

You will need

Chipboard 45cm (18in) × 35cm (14in), velvet 50cm (20in) × 40cm (16in), 491 panel pins, brown, orange, gold, blue, silver and red thread and one sheet of 2.5cm (1in) squared graph paper.

Threading the pattern
Lower branch (A)

Tie on with brown at 1A, pass to 157A, then 2A, 156A, 3A, 155A, 4A, 154A, 5A, 153A, 6A, 152A, 7A, 151A, 8A, 150A, 9A, 149A, 10A and so on in this sequence until 62A and tie off.

Top branch (A)

Tie on with brown at 101A, pass to 102A, then 100A, 103A, 99A, 104A, 98A, 105A, 97A, 106A, 96A, 107A, 95A, 108A, 94A and so on in this sequence until 38A and tie off.

Left claw (G)

Tie on with orange at 3G, pass to 9G, then 15G, 4G, 10G, 16G, 5G, 11G, 17G, 6G, 12G, 18G, 7G, 13G, 19G, 8G, 14G, 20G, 9G, 15G, 21G, pass to 3G, then 27G, 22G, 4G, 28G, 23G, 5G, 29G, 24G, 6G, 30G, 25G, 7G, 31G, 26G, 8G, 32G, 27G, 9G, 33G, pass to 40G, then 3G, 39G, 2G, 38G, 1G, 37G, 42G, 36G, 41G, 35G, 40G, 34G and tie off. Tie on at 86A, pass to 43G, then 87A, 44G, 87A, 45G, 88A, 46G, 88A, 47G and tie off.

Left leg (C)

Tie on with gold at 1C, pass to 9C, then 2C, 10C, 3C, 11C, 4C, 12C, 5C, 13C, 6C, 14C, 7C, 15C, 8C, 16C, 9C, 17C and tie off.

Right claw (H)

Tie on with orange at 1H, pass to 2H, then 9H, 3H, 10H, 4H, 11H, 5H, 12H, 6H, 13H, 7H, 14H, 8H, 15H, 9H, 16H, pass to 28H, then 17H, 27H, 18H, 26H, 19H, 25H, 20H, then 17H, 21H, 16H, 22H, 20H, 23H, 21H, 24H, 22H and tie off. Tie on at 26A, pass to 29H, then 27A,

30H, 28A, 31H, 29A, 32H, 30A, 33H and tie off.

Tail (B)

Tie on with gold at 26A, pass to 1B, then 25A, 2B, 24A, 3B, 23A, 4B, 22A, 5B, 21A, 6B, 20A, 7B, 19A and so on in this sequence until 18B and tie off. Tie on at 132A, pass to 19B, then 133A, 20B, 134A, 21B, 135A, 22B, 136A, 23B, 137A, 24B, 138A, 25B, 139A, 26B, 140A, 27B and tie off.

Lower wing (D)

Tie on with gold at 1D, pass to 21D, then 2D, 22D, 3D, 23D, 4D, 24D, 5D, 25D, 6D, 26D, 7D, 27D, 8D, 28D and so on in this sequence until 40D and tie off.

Top wing (E)

Use the same sequence as for lower wing (D).

Eye (K)

Tie on with blue at 1K, pass to 4K, then 2K, 5K, 3K, 6K and tie off.
Tie on with silver at 7K, pass to 10K, then 13K, 15K, 7K, 9K, 11K, 14K, 16K, 7K and tie off.

Beak (M & N)

Tie on with orange at 1M, pass to 2M, then 1M, 3M, 1M, 4M, 1M, 5M, 1M, 6M and so on in this sequence until 14M and tie off.
Tie on at 1N, pass to 6N, then 1N, 7N, 1N, 8N, 1N, 9N, 1N, 10N, 1N, 11N, 1N, 12N, 1N, 13N and tie off.

Body (F)

Tie on with gold at 10S, pass to 27F, then 9S, 26F, 8S, 25F, 7S, 24F, 6S, 23F, 5S, 22F, 4S, 21F, 3S, 20F, 2S, 19F, 1S, pass to 18F, then 17F, 16F, 15F, 14F, 13F, 12F, 11F, 10F, 9F, 8F, 7F and tie off. Tie on at 6F, pass to 5F, 4F, 3F, 2F, 1F and tie off. Tie on at 14E, pass to 36F, then 35F, 34F, 33F, 32F, 31F, 30F, 29F, 28F, 25W and tie off. Tie on at 1S, pass to 1J, 2J, 9N and tie off. Tie on at 1P, pass to 4J, 3J, 8M and tie off.

Cockscomb (Section P)

Tie on with gold at 1P, pass to 32P, then 40P, 32P, 41P, 32P, 25P, then 33P, 26P, 34P, 27P, 35P, 28P, 36P, 29P, 37P, 38P, 30P, 39P, 31P, 40P, 32P, and tie off.
Tie on with red at 1P, pass to 13P, then 2P, 14P, 3P, 15P, 4P, 16P, 5P, 17P, 6P, 18P, 7P, 19P, 8P, 20P, 9P, 21P, 10P, 22P, 11P, 23P, 12P, 24P, 13P, 25P, and tie off.
The remaining cockscomb sections R, T, V, X, Z, L, W are threaded in exactly the same way as Section P.

Diagram on page 41

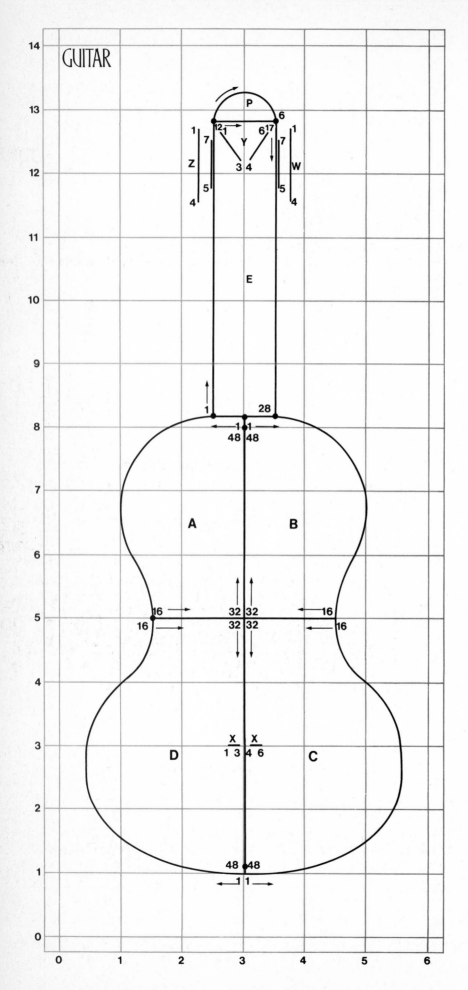

GUITAR

You will need

Chipboard 35cm (14in) × 15cm (6in), velvet 40cm (16in) × 20cm (8in), 223 panel pins, gold, silver and red thread and one sheet of 2.5cm (1in) squared graph paper.

Threading the pattern
Base

Tie on with gold at 1A, pass to 17A, then 33A, 2A, 18A, 34A, 3A, 19A, 35A, 4A, 19A, 35A and so on in this sequence until 48A, pass the thread to 1B, then 17B, 33B, 2B, 18B, 34B, 3B, 19B, 35B, 4B, 20B, 36B and so on in this sequence until 48B, pass the thread to 1C, then 17C, 33C, 2C, 18C, 33C, 3C, 19C, 35C, 4C, 20C, 35C and so on in this sequence until 48C, pass the thread to 1D, then 17D 33D, 2D, 18D, 34D, 3D, 19D, 35D, 4D, 19D, 35D and so on in this sequence until 48D and tie off.

Neck

Tie on with silver at 1E, pass to 2E, then 27E, 26E, 3E, 4E, 25E, 24E, 5E, 6E, 23E, 22E, 7E, 8E, 21E, 20E, 9E, 10E, 19E, 18E, 11E, 12E, then 17E, 18E, 11E, 10E, 19E, 20E, 9E, 8E, 21E, 22E, 7E, 6E, 23E, 24E, 5E, 4E, 25E, 26E, 3E, 2E, 27E, 28E and tie off.

Tie on with gold at 1A, pass to 1E, then 2E, 3E, 4E, 5E and so on in this sequence until 5Z, then pass the thread to 3Z, then 4Z, 5Z, 6Z, 2Z, 3Z, 6Z, 7Z, 1Z, 2Z, 7Z, 12E, then 2P, 13E, 3P, 14E, 4P, 15E, 5P, 16E, 6P, 17E, then 6P, 5P, 4P, 3P, 2P, 1P, then 17E, 7W, then 2W, 1W, 7W, 6W, 3W, 2W, 6W, 5W, 4W, 3W, 5W and tie off.

Tie on at 28E, pass to 27E, then 26E, 25E, 24E and so on in this sequence until 5W and tie off.

Strings

Tie on with red at 1X, pass to 1Y, then 2X, 2Y, 3X, 3Y, 4X, 4Y, 5X, 5Y, 6X, 6Y and tie off.

STOCK CAR

You will need

Chipboard 60cm (24in) × 30cm (12in), velvet 65cm (26in) × 35cm (14in), 210 panel pins, gold, turquoise, brown, silver and lime green thread and one sheet of 2.5cm (1in) squared graph paper.

Threading the pattern
Bodywork

Tie on with turquoise at Nail H, pass to 20J, H, 19J, H, 18J, H, 17J, H, 16J, then pass to 21G, 15J, 20G, 14J, 19G, 13J, 18G, 12J, 17G, 11J, 16G, 10J, 15G, 9J, 14G, 8J, 13G, 7J,

12G, 11G, 6J, 10G, 9G, 5J, 8G, 7G, 4J, 6G, 5G, 3J, 4G, 3G, 2J, 2G, 1G, 1J and tie off. Tie on with turquoise at 1T, pass to X, then 1T, pass to 1M, 1T, 2M, 1T, 3M, 1T, 4M, 1L, 4M, then 2L, 5M, 3L, 6M, 4L, 7M, 5L, 8M, 6L, 9M, 7L and so on in this sequence until 27M, then pass to 10J, then 28M, 9J, 29M, 8J, 30M, 7J, 31M, 6J, 32M, 5J, 33M, 4J, 34M, 3J, 35M, 2J, 36M, 1J, 37M, 1J, 38M, 1J, 39M and tie off.

Tie on with gold at 1C, pass to 1P, then 2C, 2P, 3C, 3P, 4C, 4P and tie off.

Tie on with gold at 1N, pass to 1Q, then 2N, 2Q, 3N, 3Q, 4N, 4Q, 5N, 5Q and tie off. Tie on with gold at 1A, pass to 1B, then 2A, 2B, 3A, 3B, 4A, 4B, then 4A, 1F, 1E, Z, 2E, 21G, 3E, 1E, 2F, 2E, 1F, 4A and tie off.

Steering wheel (K)

Tie on with brown at 1K, pass to 7K, then 13K, 2K, 8K, 14K, 3K, 9K, 15K, 4K, 10K, 16K, 5K, 11K, 17K, 6K, 12K, 18K, 13K, 14J, 13K and tie off.

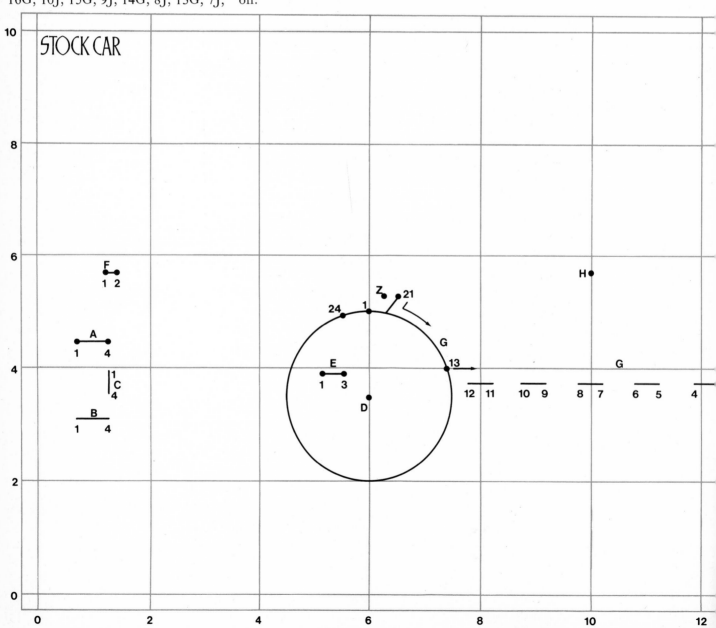

Wheels (R)

Tie on with silver at centre pin R, pass to 1R, R, 3R, R, 5R, R, 7R, R, 9R and so on in this sequence until 23R, then R and tie off.

Tie on with lime at 1R, pass to 9R, then 2R, 10R, 3R, 11R, 4R, 12R, 5R, 13R, 6R, 14R, 7R, 15R, 8R, 16R and so on in this sequence until 1R again and tie off.

Repeat for Wheel D.

Cut 10cm (4in) of lime thread, fold in shape of a figure 4 and stick onto threads of the car bonnet.

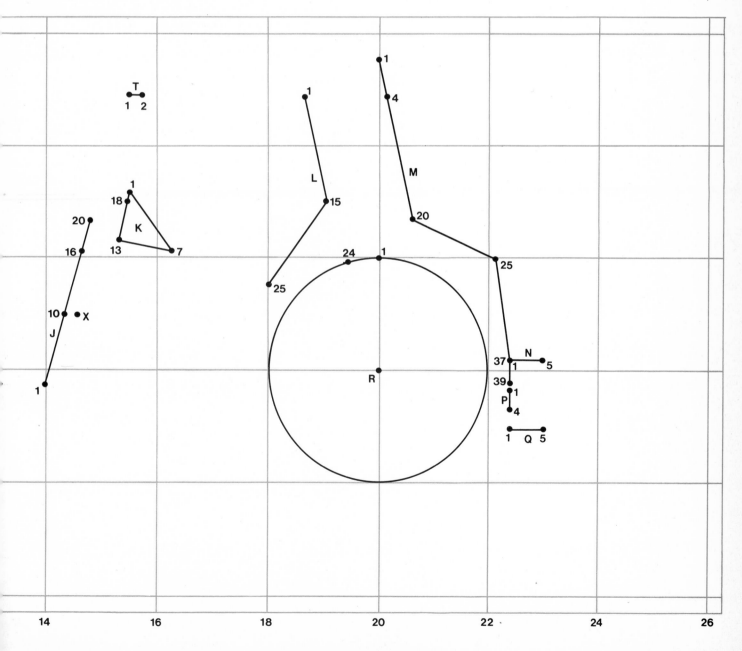

Instructions on page 46–47

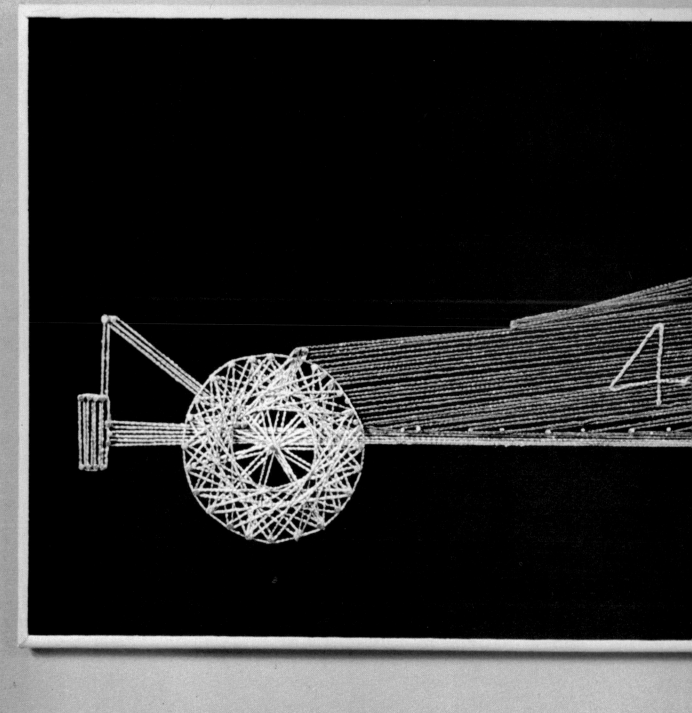

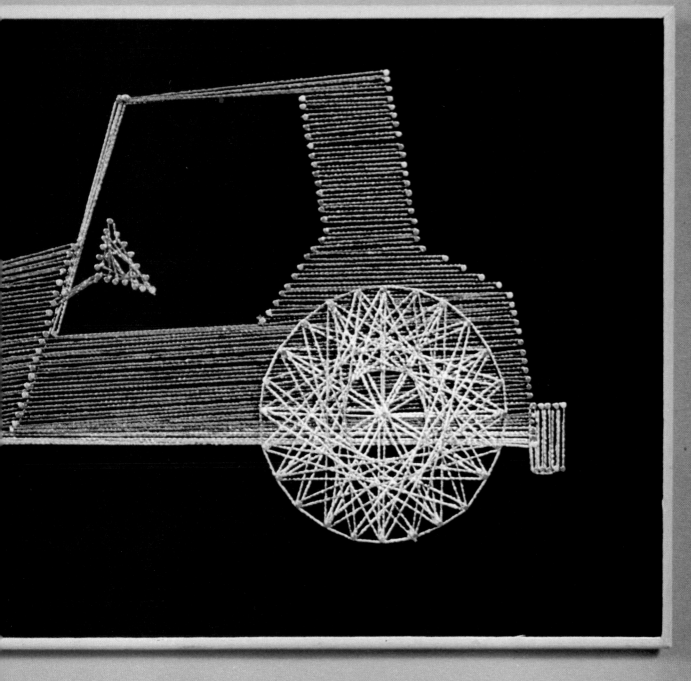

50

MERMAID

You will need

Chipboard 70cm (28in) × 50cm (20in), velvet 72.5cm (29in) × 52.5cm (21in), 715 panel pins, green, turquoise, silver, gold and red thread and one sheet of 2.5cm (1in) squared graph paper.

Threading the pattern
Tail (A)

Tie on with turquoise at 1A, pass to 2A, 3A, 4A, 5A, 6A, 7A, 8A, 9A, then 10A, 8A, 12A, 6A, 14A, 4A, 16A, 2A, 18A, then 19A, 17A, 21A, 15A, 23A, 13A, 25A, 11A, 27A, then 28A, 26A, 30A, 24A, 32A, 22A, 34A, 20A, 36A and so on in this sequence until 162A and tie off.

Tie on with silver at 9A, pass to 11A, then 7A, 13A, 5A, 15A, 3A, 17A, 1A, 18A, 20A, 16A, 22A, 14A, 24A, 12A, 26A, 10A, 27A, 29A, 25A, 31A, 23A, 33A, 21A, 35A, 19A, 36A and so on in this sequence until 154A and tie off.

Tail fin (B)

Tie on with silver at 1B, pass to 15B, then 3B, 17B, 5B, 19B, 7B, 21B, 9B, 23B, 11B, 25B, 13B, 27B, 15B, 1B and tie off.

Tie on with turquoise at 2B, pass to 16B, then 4B, 18B, 6B, 20B, 8B, 22B, 10B, 24B, 12B, 26B, 14B, 28B, 16B, 2B and tie off.

Tail fin (C)

Tie on with silver at 1C, pass to 14C, then 3C, 16C, 5C, 18C, 7C, 20C, 9C, 22C, 11C, 24C, 13C, 26C, 14C, 2C and tie off.

Tie on with turquoise at 2C, pass to 15C, then 4C, 17C, 6C, 19C, 8C, 21C, 10C, 23C, 12C, 25C, 14C, 1C and tie off.

Water droplet (U)

Tie on with turquoise at 1U, pass to 7U, then 12U, 6U, 11U, 5U, 10U, 4U, 9U, 3U, 8U, 2U, 7U, 1U and tie off.
Repeat for water droplets S and T.

Bra (Part Z)

Tie on with turquoise at 17Z, pass to 1Z, then 17Z, 2Z, 17Z, 3Z, 17Z, 4Z, 17Z, 5Z, 17Z, 6Z, 17Z and so on in this sequence until 16Z, pass to 17Z and tie off.
Repeat for Part D.

Bra (Part G)

Tie on with turquoise at 1G, pass to 7G, then 2G, 8G, 3G, 9G, 4G, 10G, 5G, 11G, 6G, 12G and tie off.

Bra (Part F)

Tie on with turquoise at 1F, pass to 8F, then 2F, 9F, 3F, 10F, 4F, 11F, 5F, 12F, 6F, 13F, 7F, 14F and tie off.

Hair (H)

Tie on with gold at 1H, pass to 77H, then 2H, 76H, 3H, 75H, 4H, 74H, 5H, 73H, 6H, 72H, 7H, 71H, 8H, 70H, 9H and so on in this sequence until 38H and tie off.

Hair (N)

Tie on with gold at 1N, pass to 34N, then 2N, 33N, 3N, 32N, 4N, 31N, 5N, 30N, 6N, 29N, 7N, 28N, 8N, 27N and so on in this sequence until 19N and tie off.

Hair (P)

Tie on with gold at 18P, pass to 20P, then 17P, 21P, 16P, 22P, 15P, 23P, 14P, 24P, 5P, 25P, 2P, 1P and tie off.
Tie on at 14P, pass to 6P, then 13P, 9P, 10P, 12P, 11P and tie off.

Hair (Q)

Tie on with gold at 1Q, pass to 16Q, then 2Q, 15Q, 3Q, 14Q, 4Q, 13Q, 5Q, 12Q, 6Q, 11Q, 7Q, 10Q, 8Q, 9Q and tie off.

Mouth (J)

Tie on with red at 1J, pass to 7J, then 2J, 8J, 3J, 9J, 4J, 10J, 5J, 11J, 6J, 12J, 7J, 1J and tie off.

Eye (M)

Tie on with silver at 1M, pass to 5M, then 2M, 6M, 3M, 7M, 4M, 8M, 5M, 1M and tie off.
Repeat for Eye L.

Eyebrow (M)

Tie on with brown at 9M, pass to 10M, then 11M, 12M, 13M, 14M and tie off.
Repeat for Eyebrow L.

Jug (R)

Tie on with green at 1R, pass to 10R, 2R, 11R, 3R, 12R, 4R, 13R, 5R, 14R, 6R, 15R, 7R, 16R, 8R, 17R, 9R, 18R, then 19R, 20R, 21R, 22R, 23R, 24R, 25R, 1R, then 26R, 27R, 28R, 29R, 30R, 31R, 32R, 33R, 34R, 35R, 36R and so on in this sequence until 70R, pass to 73R, 71R, 74R, 72R, 75R, 73R, 76R, 74R, 77R and so on in this sequence until 70R, then pass around full outline of jug passing from nail to nail.

Arms outline (V, W, X, Y)

Tie on with silver at 1V, pass to 2V, then 3V, 4V, 5V, 6V, 7V and so on in this sequence until the outline is completed.
Repeat for W, X, Y.

Diagram on page 52

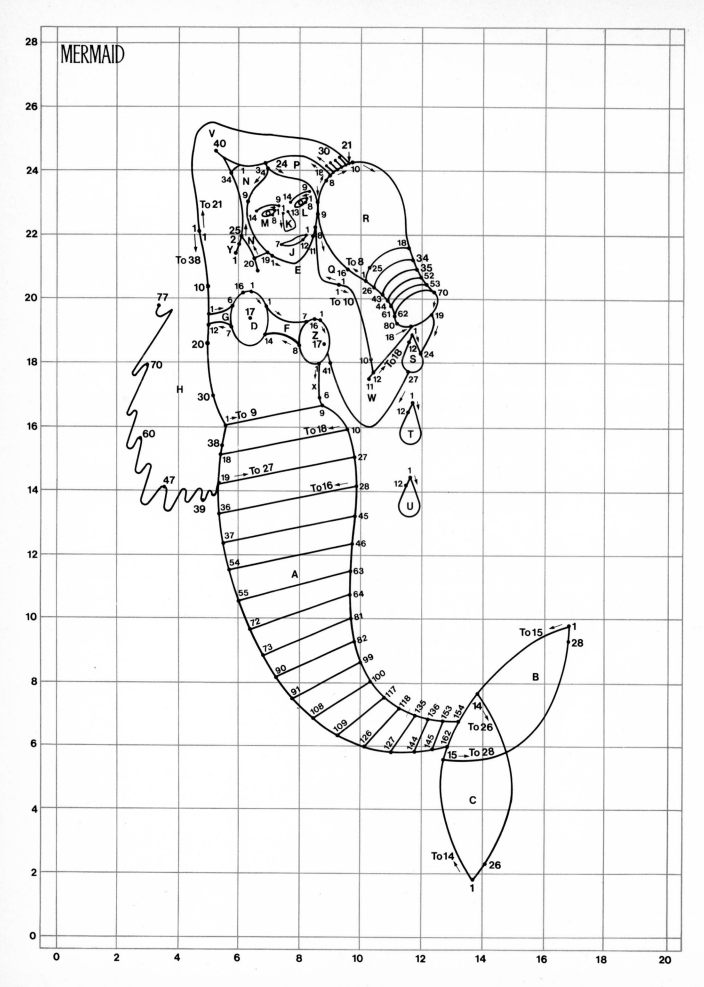

MERMAID

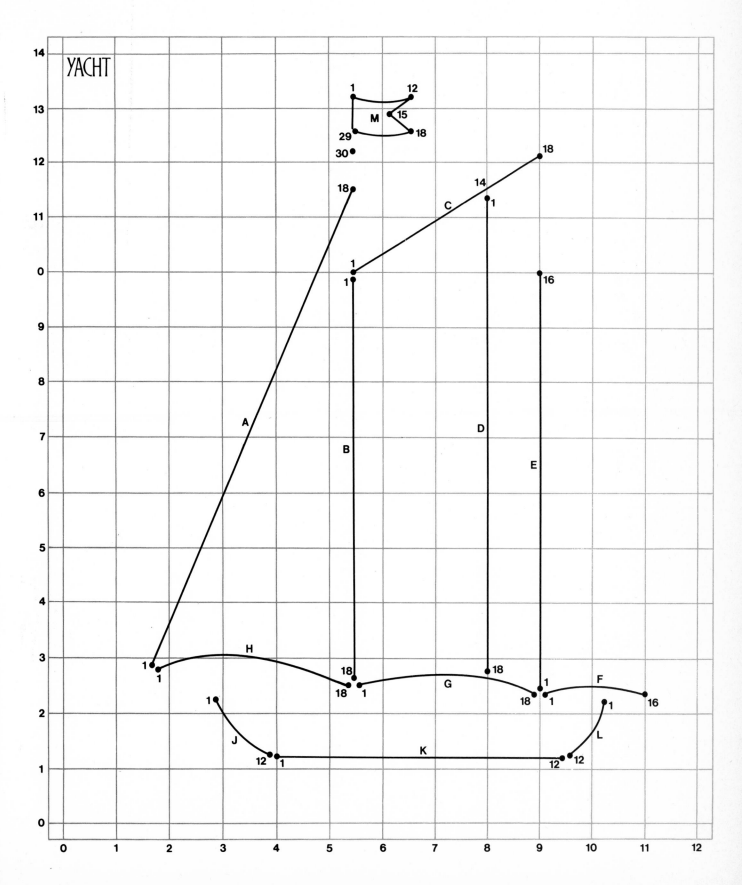

YACHT

53

54

YACHT

You will need

Chipboard 35cm (14in) × 30cm (12in), velvet 40cm (16in) × 35cm (14in), 208 panel pins, green, red and gold thread and one sheet of 2.5cm (1in) squared graph paper.

Threading the pattern
Base (J, K & L)

Tie on with green at 1J, pass to 1L, then 2J, 2L, 3J, 3L, 4J, 4L, 5J, 5L, 6J, 6L, 7J, 7L, 8J, 8L, 9J, 9L, 10J, 10L. 11J, 11L, 12J, 12L, pass to 6K, then 11L, 7K, 10L, 8K, 9L, 9K, 8L, 10K, 7L, 11K, 6L, 12K, pass to 6K, then 12J, 6K, 11J, 5K, 10J, 5K, 9J, 4K, 8J, 4K, 7J, 3K, 6J, 3K, 5J, 2K, 4J, 2K, 3J, 1K, 2J, 1K, 1J and tie off.

Front sail (A, H)

Tie on with gold at 18A, pass to 4H, then 18A, 5H, 18A, 6H, 18A, 7H, 18A, 8H and so on in this sequence until 18H, pass to 18A, then 1H, 17A, 2H, 16A, 3H, 15A, 4H, 14A, 5H, 13A and so on in this sequence until 18H and tie off.

Middle sail (B, C, D & G)

Tie on with gold at 1C, pass to 1G, then 2C, 2G, 3C, 3G, 4C, 4G, 5C, 5G, 6C, 6G, 7C, 7G and so on in this sequence until 14G, then pass to 9D, then 14G, 10D, 15G, 11D, 15G, 12D, 16G, 13D, 16G, 14D, 17G, 15D, 17G, 16D, 18G, 17D, 18G, 18D, pass to 9D, then 14C, 8D, 14C, 7D, 15C, 6D, 15C, 5D, 16C, 4D, 16C, 3D, 17C, 2D, 17C, 1D, 18C, pass to 1B, then 17C, 2B, 16C, 3B, 15C, 4B, 14C, 5B, 13C, 6B, 12C, 7B, 11C, 8B, 10C, 9B and so on in this sequence until 18B, pass to 1B, then 1G, 2B, 2G, 3B, 3G, 4B, 4G, 5B, 5G, 6B, 6G, 7B, 7G and so on in this sequence until 18G and tie off.

Rear sail

Tie on with gold at 1F, pass to 16E, then 2F, 16E, 3F, 16E, 4F, 16E, 5F, 16E, 6F, 16E and so on in this sequence until 16F, then pass to 1F, then 15E, 2F, 14E, 3F, 13E, 4F, 12E, 5F, 11E, 6F, 10E, 7F, 9E and so on in this sequence until 16F and tie off.

Flag (M)

Tie on with red at 1M, pass to 30M, then 2M, 29M, 3M, 28M, 4M, 27M, 5M, 26M, 6M, 25M, 7M, 24M, 8M, 23M, 9M, 22M, 15M, 21M, 16M, 20M, 17M, 19M, 18M, then 15M, 12M, 13M, 11M, 14M, 10M, 15M and tie off.

Rigging

Tie on with gold at 1M, pass to 18A, then 1M, and tie off.
Tie on with green at 1J, pass to 1A and tie off. Tie on at 1L, pass to 16F and tie off.

Diagram on page 53

CANADIAN PACIFIC

You will need

Chipboard 90cm (36in) × 30cm (12in), velvet 95cm (38in) × 35cm (14in), 967 panel pins, blue, red, orange, silver, brown and gold thread and one sheet of 2.5cm (1in) squared graph paper.

Threading the pattern
Train base plate (B)

Tie on with brown at 1B, pass to 10B, then 2B, 9B, 3B, 8B, 4B, 5B, 6B and tie off.

Coal carrier (E)

Tie on with blue at 1E, pass to 40E, then 2E, 39E, 3E, 38E, 4E, 37E, 5E, 36E, 6E, 35E, 7E and so on in this sequence until 17E and tie off.
Tie on with red at 20E, pass to 21E, then 19E, 22E, 18E, 23E, 17E, 24E and tie off.

Coal carrier wheels and wheel-braces (W)

Tie on with orange at 1W, pass to 9W, then 16W, 8W, 15W, 7W, 14W, 6W, 13W, 5W, 12W, 4W, 11W, 3W, 10W, 2W, 9W, 1W, then pass to 5W, then 2W, 6W, 3W, 7W, 4W, 8W, 5W, 9W, 6W, 10W, 7W, 11W and so on in this sequence until 5W again and tie off.
Repeat for other three wheels.
Tie on with silver at 17W, pass to 26W, then 18W, 25W, 19W, 24W, 20W, 23W, 21W, 22W and tie off.
Repeat for other wheelbrace.

Letter C

Tie on with silver at 1C, pass to 2C, 3C, 4C, 5C, 6C, 7C, 8C, 9C, 10C, 11C and so on in this sequence until 20C, then on opposite side of the nails, 19C, 18C, 17C, 16C, 15C, 14C, 13C, 12C, 11C, 10C and so on in this sequence until 1C and tie off.

Letter P

Tie on with silver at 1P, pass to 2P, 3P, 4P, 5P, 6P, 7P, 8P, 9P, 10P, 11P, 12P, 2P, then on opposite side of the nails, 12P, 11P, 10P, 9P, 8P, 7P, 6P, 5P, 4P, 3P, 2P, 1P and tie off.

Letter R

Tie on with silver at 1R, pass to 2R, 3R, 4R, 5R, 6R, 7R, 8R, 9R, 10R, 11R, 12R, 13R, 12R, 2R, then on opposite side of the nails, 12R, 11R, 10R, 9R, 8R, 7R, 6R, 5R, 4R, 3R, 2R, 1R, and tie off.
Repeat for other R.

Continued over

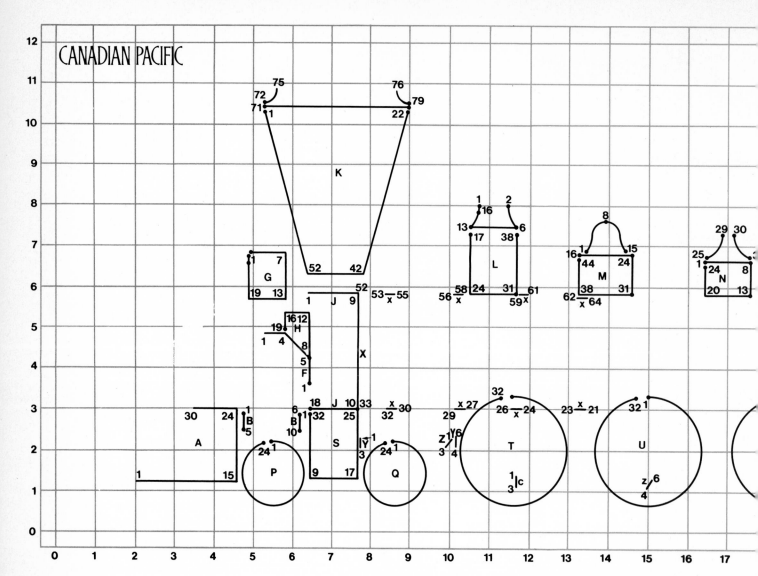

CANADIAN PACIFIC

Cab (D)

Tie on with blue at 1D, pass to 56D, 2D, 55D, 3D, 54D, 4D, 53D, 5D, 52D, 6D, 51D, 7D, 50D, 8D, 49D, 9D, 48D, then 72D, 47D, 71D, 46D, 70D, 45D, 69D, 44D, 68D, 43D, 67D, 42D, 66D, 41D, 65D, 40D, then 18D, 39D, 19D, 38D, 20D, 37D, 21D, 36Đ, 22D, 35D, 23D, 34D, 24D, 33D, 25D, 32D, 26D, 31D, 27D, 30D, 28D, 29D and tie off.
Tie on at 10D, pass to 57D, then 11D, 58D, 12D, 59D, 13D, 60D, 14D, 61D, 15D, 62D, 16D, 63D, 17D, 64D, 18D and tie off.

Water container (X)

Tie on with blue at 1X, pass to 52X, then 2X, 51X, 3X, 50X, 4X, 49X, 5X, 48X, 6X, 47X, 7X and so on in this sequence until 33X and tie off.
Tie on with gold at 53X, pass to 32X, then 54X, 31X, 55X, 30X, and tie off. Tie on at 56X, pass to 29X, then

57X, 28X, 58X, 27X and tie off. Tie on at 59X, pass to 26X, then 60X, 25X, 61X, 24X and tie off. Tie on at 62X, pass to 23X, then 63X, 22X, 64X, 21X and tie off.
Tie on with silver at 6X, pass to 47X, then 7X, 46X and tie off.
Tie on with red at 1J, pass to 18J, then 2J, 17J, 3J, 16J, 4J, 15J, 5J, 14J, 6J, 13J, 7J, 12J, 8J, 11J, 9J, 10J and tie off.

Large chimney (K)

Tie on with gold at 76K, pass to 75K, then 77K, 74K, 78K, 73K, 79K, 72K, 22K, 1K and tie off.
Tie on with silver at 2J, pass to 50K, then 3J, 49K, 4J, 48K, 5J, 47K, 6J, 46K, 7J, 45K, 8J, 44K and tie off.
Tie on at 1K, pass to 22K, then 42K, 52K, 2K, 23K, 42K, 53K, 3K, 24K, 43K, 54K, 4K, 25K, 43K, 55K, 5K, 26K, 44K, 56K, 6K, 27K, 44K, 57K and so on in this sequence until 71K

and tie off. *Note* Nails between 42K and 52K are passed twice.

Small chimney (L)

Tie on with gold at 1L, pass to 2L, then 16L, 3L, 15L, 4L, 14L, 5L, 13L, 6L and tie off.
Tie on with blue at 6L, pass to 21L, then 7L, 22L, 8L, 23L, 9L, 24L, 10L, 25L, 11L, 26L, 12L, 27L, 13L, 28L, 17L, 29L, 18L, 30L, 19L, 31L and so on in this sequence until 6L again and tie off.

Bell chimney (M)

Tie on with gold at 1M, pass to 15M, then 2M, 14M, 3M, 13M, 4M, 12M, 5M, 11M, 6M, 10M, 7M, 9M, 8M, and tie off.
Tie on with blue at 19M, pass to 7M, then 20M, 8M, 21M, 9M and tie off. Tie on at 16M, pass to 31M, then 17M, 32M, 18M, 33M, 19M, 34M, 20M, 35M, 21M, 36M and so

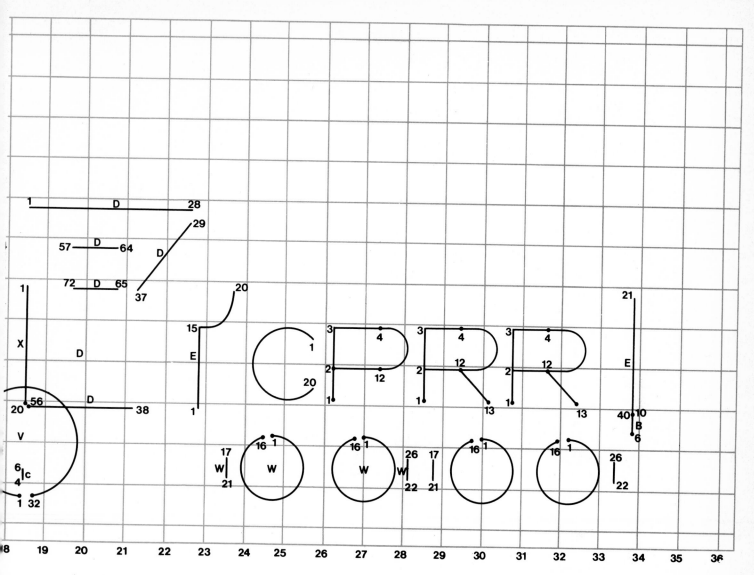

on in this sequence until 16M again and tie off.

Small chimney (N)

Tie on with gold at 29N, pass to 30N, then 28N, 31N, 27N, 32N, 26N, 33N, 25N, 34N, 1N, 8N and tie off.
Tie on with blue at 1N, pass to 13N, then 2N, 14N, 3N, 15N, 4N, 16N, 5N, 17N, 6N, 18N, 7N, 19N, 8N, 20N, 9N, 21N, 10N, 22N, 11N, 23N, 12N, 24N, 13N, 1N and tie off.

Lantern (G)

Tie on with gold at 1G, pass to 7G, then 13G, 19G, 2G, 8G, 14G, 20G, 3G, 9G, 15G, 21G, 4G, 10G, 16G, 22G and so on in this sequence until 24G and tie off.

Lantern bracket (H)

Tie on with silver at 16G, pass to 1H, then 15G, 2H, 14G, 3H, 13G, 4H, then pass to 8H, 12H, 16H, 5H, 9H, 13H, 17H, 6H, 10H, 14H, 18H, 7H, 11H, 15H, 19H and tie off.

Bumper bracket (F)

Tie on with silver at 1F, pass to 24A, then 2F, 25A, 3F, 26A, 4F, 27A, 5F, 28A and tie off.

Bumper (A)

Tie on with silver at 1A, pass to 30A, then 2A, 29A, 3A, 28A, 4A, 27A, 5A, 26A, 6A, 25A, 7A, 24A and so on in this sequence until 15A and tie off.

Small wheels (P)

Tie on with orange at 1P, pass to 13P, then 24P, 12P, 23P, 11P, 22P, 10P, 21P, 9P, 20P, 8P and so on in this sequence until 24P, pass to 7P, then 1P, 8P, 2P, 9P, 3P, 10P, 4P, 11P, 5P, 12P, 6P, and so on in this sequence until 7P again and tie off.
Repeat for wheel Q.

Large wheel (T)

Tie on with orange at 1T, pass to 17T, then 32T, 16T, 31T, 15T, 30T, 14T, 29T, 13T, 28T, 12T and so on in this sequence until 32T, pass to 9T, then 1T, 10T, 2T, 11T, 3T, 12T, 4T, 13T, 5T, 14T, 6T, 15T and so on in this sequence until 9T again and tie off.
Repeat for Wheels U and V.

Piston chambers (S)

Tie on with gold at 1S, pass to 17S, then 2S, 18S, 3S, 19S, 4S, 20S, 5S, 21S, 6S, 22S, 7S, 23S and so on in this sequence until 1S again and tie off.

Con rods (Y, Z, & C)

Tie on with silver at 1Y, pass to 6Y, then 2Y, 5Y, 3Y, 4Y, pass to 1Z, then 6Z, 2Z, 5Z, 3Z, 4Z, 6Z, pass to 1C, then 6C, 2C, 5C, 3C, 4C and tie off.

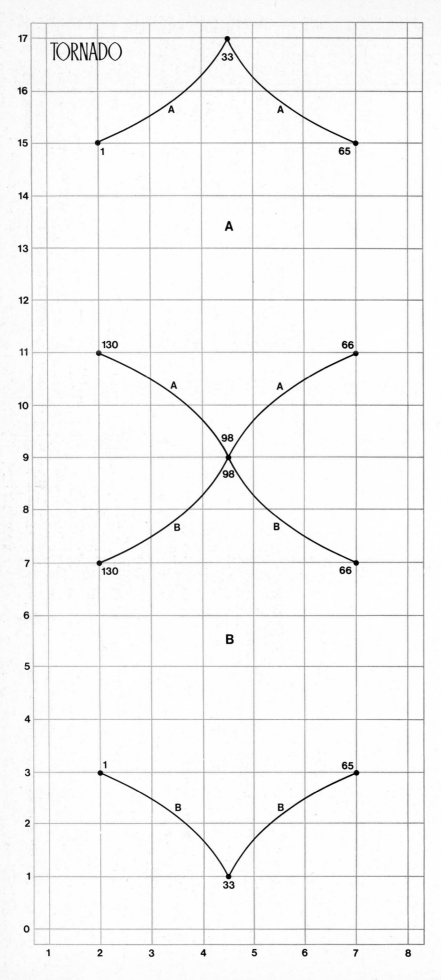

TORNADO

You will need

Chipboard 85cm (34in) × 30cm (12in), velvet 90cm (36in) × 35cm (14in), 260 panel pins, red and orange thread and one sheet of 2.5cm (1in) squared graph paper.

Threading the pattern

Tie on with red at 1A, pass to 66B, then 2A, 67B, 3A, 68B, 4A, 69B, 5A, 70B, 6A, 71B, 7A, 72B, 8A, 73B and so on in this sequence until 130B and tie off. Tie on with red at 1B, pass to 66A, then 2B, 67A, 3B, 68A, 4B, 69A, 5B, 70A, 6B, 71A, 7B, 72A, 8B, 73A and so on in this sequence until 130A and tie off.

Tie on with orange at 1A, pass to 66A, then 2A, 67A, 3A, 68A, 4A, 69A, 5A, 70A, 6A, 71A, 7A, 72A, 8A, 73A and so on in this sequence until 130A and tie off. Tie on with orange at 1B, pass to 66B, then 2B, 67B, 3B, 68B, 4B, 69B, 5B, 70B, 6B, 71B, 7B, 72B, 8B, 73B and so on in this sequence until 130B and tie off.

Instructions on page 66

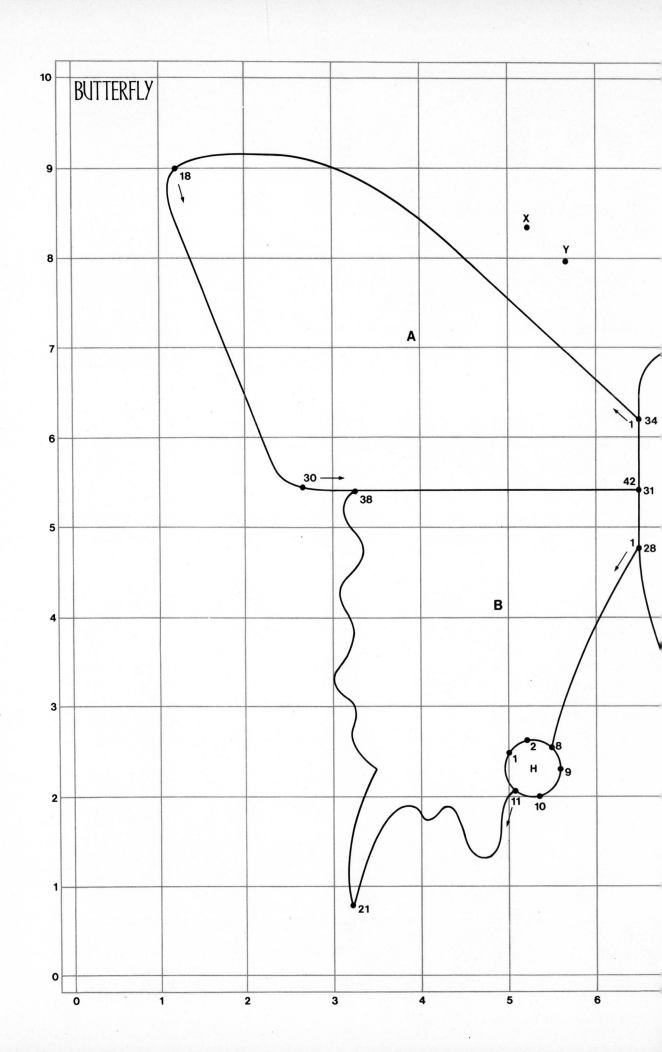

BUTTERFLY

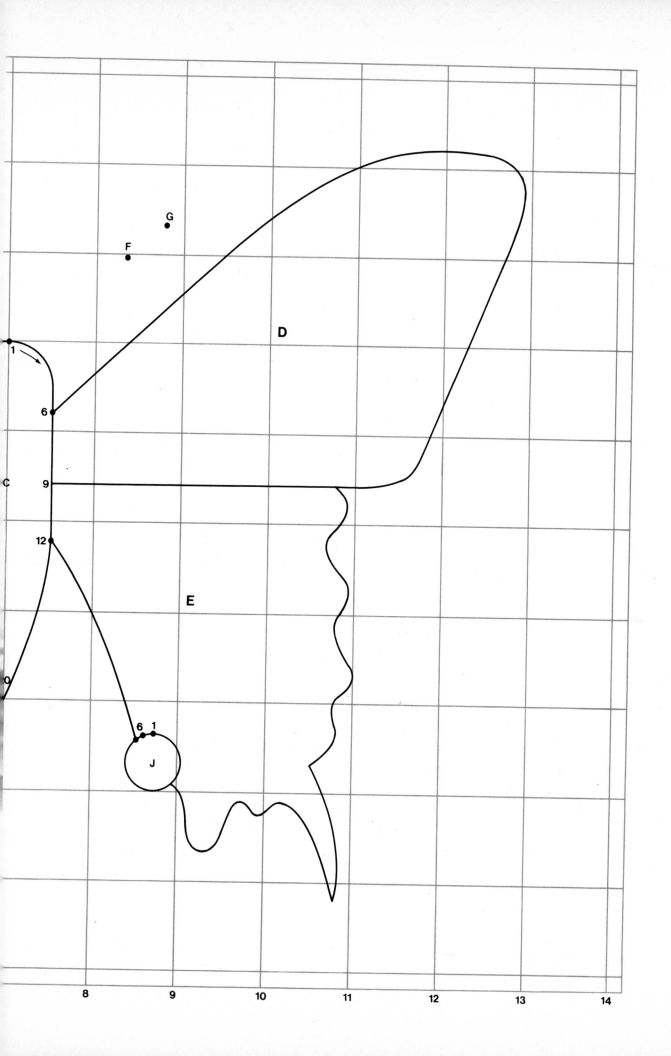

BUTTERFLY

You will need
Chipboard 35cm (14in) × 25cm (10in), velvet 40cm (16in) × 30cm (12in), 214 panel pins, gold and lime green thread and one sheet of 2.5cm (1in) squared graph paper.

Threading the pattern
Left feeler
Tie on with gold at 37C, pass to Y, then X, Y, X again and tie off.

Right feeler
Tie on with gold at 3C, pass to F, then G, F, G again and tie off.

Body
Tie on with gold at 20C, pass to 1C, then 19C, 38C, 18C, 37C, 17C, 36C, 16C, 35C, 15C, 34C, 14C, 33C and so on in this sequence until 20C again and tie off.

Left wing
Tie on with gold at 31C, pass to 19A, then 31C, 20A, 32C, 21A, 33C, 22A, 34C, 23A, 1A, 24A, 2A, 25A, 3A, 26A, 4A, 27A, 5A, 28A, 6A, 29A, 7A, 30A and so on in this sequence until 41A, pass to 21B, then 40A, 20B, 39A, 19B, 38A, 18B, 37A, 17B, 36A, 16B, 35A, 15B, 34A, 14B, 33A, 13B, 38B, 12B, 37B, 11B, 36B, 10B, 35B and so on in this sequence until 41A again and tie off.
Tie on with green at 1A, pass to 12A, then 1A, 13A, 2A, 14A, 3A, 15A, 4A, 16A, 5A, 17A, 6A, 18A and so on in this sequence until 41A, pass to 38B, then 40A, 37B, 39A, 36B, 38A, 35B, 37A, 34B, 36A, 33B, 35A, 32B, 34A, 31B and tie off. Tie on at 1H, pass to 9B, then 2H, 10B, 8B, 11B, 9B, 1H, 2H, 8B, 9B, 10B, 2H and tie off.

Right wing
As left wing.

Diagram on page 64-65

CLOCK

You will need
Chipboard 45cm (18in) × 25cm (10in), velvet 50cm (20in) × 30cm (12in), 12 gold and 390 silver coloured panel pins, gold, silver and red thread and one sheet of 2.5cm (1in) squared graph paper. On the diagram Section E (clock-face minute markers) is made up of 60 panel pins and Nos. 5, 10, 15, 20, 25, 30, 35, 40, 45, 50, 55, 60 are gold headed panel pins.

Threading the pattern
Tie on with silver at 1A, pass to 9A, then 17A, 2A, 10A, 18A, 3A, 11A, 19A, 4A, 12A, 20A, 5A, 13A, 21A, 6A, 14A, 22A, 7A, 15A, 23A, 8A, 16A, 24A then pass to 1A, then 1C, 9C, 17C, 2C, 10C, 18C, 3C, 11C, 19C, 4C, 12C, 20C, 5C, 13C, 21C, 6C, 14C, 22C, 7C, 15C, 23C, 8C, 16C, 24C, pass to 17C, then 17D, 1D, 9D, 17D, 2D, 10D, 18D, 3D, 11D, 19D, 4D, 12D, 20D, 5D, 13D, 21D, 6D, 14D, 22D, 7D, 15D, 23D, 8D, 16D, 24D, pass to 1D, then 1B, 9B, 17B, 2B, 10B, 18B, 3B, 11B, 19B, 4B, 12B, 20B, 5B, 13B, 21B, 6B, 14B, 22B, 7B, 15B, 23B, 8B, 16B, 24B, then 17B, 17A, 9A, 9C, 9D, 9B, 9A and tie off.

Tie on at W, pass to X, then Y, Z, W, X, Y, Z, W and tie off. (This is threaded in silver).
Tie on with gold at 1H, pass to 6H, then 2H, 5H, 3H, 4H and tie off.
Tie on with gold at 1J, pass to 13J, then 2J, 14J, 3J, 15J, 4J, 16J and so on in this sequence until 1J again and tie off.
Tie on with red at 1F, pass to 7F, then 2F, 8F, 3F, 9F, 4F, 10F, 5F, 11F, 6F, 12F, 1F, pass to 8G, then 2G, 9G, 3G, 10G, 4G, 11G, 5G, 12G, 6G, 13G, 7G, 14G, 1G and tie off.

Diagram on page 68

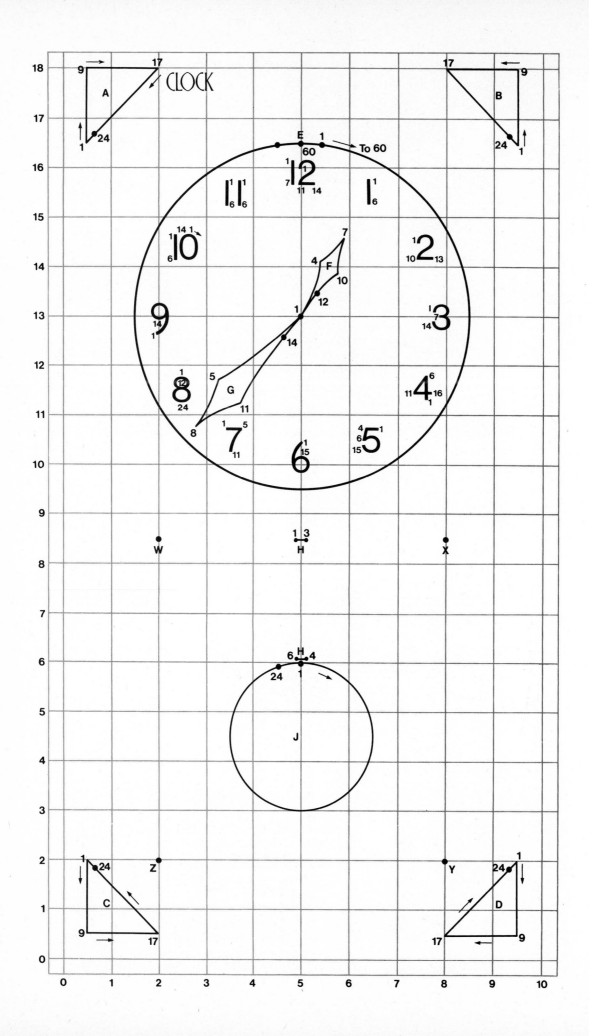

CLOCK

PEACOCK

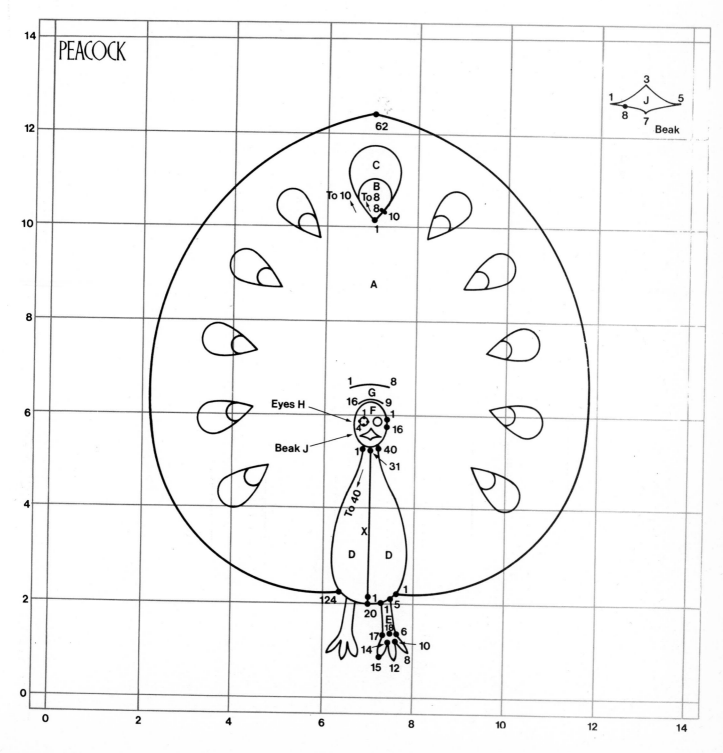

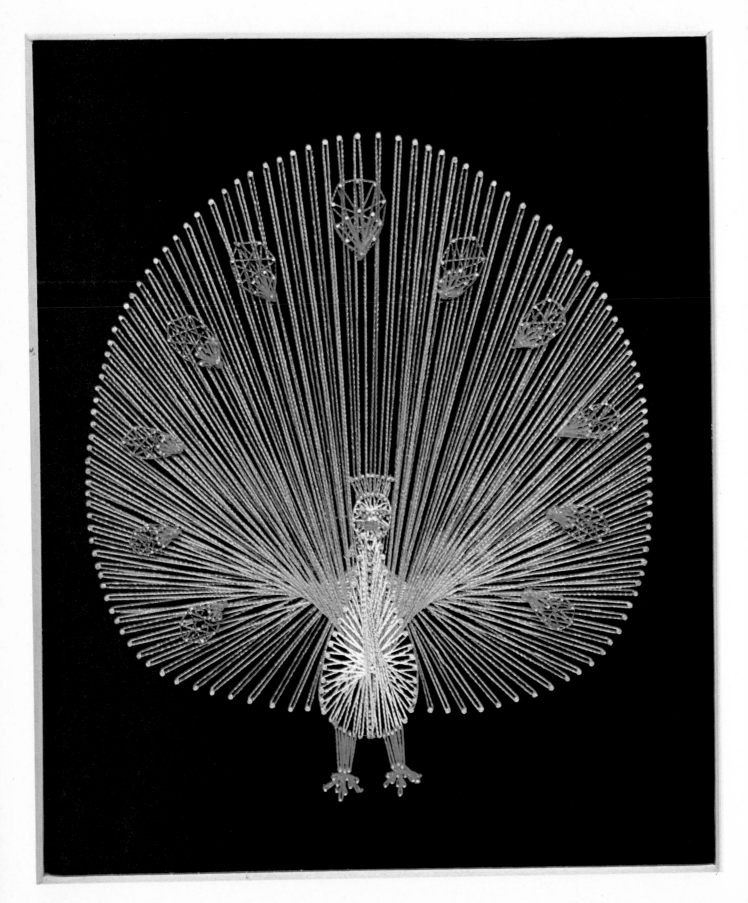

70

PEACOCK

You will need
Chipboard 35cm (14in) × 30cm (12in), velvet 40cm (16in) × 35cm (14in), 432 panel pins, red, turquoise, blue, orange and green thread and one sheet of 2.5cm (1in) squared graph paper.

Threading the pattern
Tail
Tie on with orange at 31X, pass to 1A, then 31X, 2A, 30X, 3A, 30X, 4A, 29X, 5A, 29X, 6A, 28X, 7A, 28X and so on in this sequence until 62A and tie off. Tie on at 31X, pass to 124A, then 31X, 123A, 30X, 122A, 30X, 121A, 29X, 120A, 29X, 119A, 28X, 118A, 28X, and so on in this sequence until 62A and tie off.

Tail patterning
Tie on with red at 1B, pass to 2B, then 1B, 3B, 1B, 4B, 1B, 5B, 1B, 6B, 1B, 7B, 1B, 8B then 1B and tie off.

Tie on with blue at 1C, pass to 6C, then 2C, 7C, 3C, 8C, 4C, 9C, 5C, 10C, then 1C, 2C, 3C, 4C, 5C, 6C, 7C, 8C, 9C, 10C, and tie off.
Repeat for other tail patterns.

Body
Tie on with silver at 1D, pass to 21D, then 2D, 22D, 3D, 23D, 4D, 24D, 5D, 25D, 6D, 26D, 7D, 27D, 8D, 28D and so on in this sequence until 40D and tie off.

Legs and claws
Tie on with red at 1E, pass to 17E, then 2E, 18E, 3E, 18E, 4E, 6E, 5E, 6E, then pass to 14E, 6E, 15E, 6E, 16E, 18E, then 11E, 18E, 12E, 18E, 13E, 17E, then 7E, 17E, 8E, 17E, 9E, 17E and tie off.
Repeat for other leg.

Head
Tie on with silver at 1F, pass to 9F,

then 16F, 8F 15F, 7F, 14F, 6F and so on in this sequence until 1F again and tie off.

Cockscomb
Tie on with turquoise at 1G, pass to 16G, then 2G, 15G, 3G, 14G, 4G, 13G, 5G, 12G, 6G, 11G, 7G, 10G, 8G, 9G, and tie off.

Eyes
Tie on with green at 1H, pass to 3H, then 1H, 2H, 3H, 4H, 2H, 4H, 1H and tie off.
Repeat for other eye.

Beak
Tie on with red at 1J, pass to 5J, then 8J, 4J, 7J, 3J, 6J, 2J, 5J, 1J and tie off.

Diagram on page 69

QUADPACK

You will need
Chipboard 37.5cm (15in) × 37.5cm (15in), velvet 42.5cm (17in) × 42.5cm (17in), 168 panel pins, orange thread and one sheet of 2.5cm (1in) squared graph paper.

Threading the pattern
Tie on with orange at 1B, pass to 1F, then 2B, 2F, 3B, 3F, 4B, 4F, 5B, 5F, 6B, 6F, 7B, 7F, 8B, 8F, 9B, 9F, 10B, 10F, 11B, 11F, 12B, 12F, 13B, 13F, 14B, 14F and tie off.
Tie on at 1A, pass to 1E, 2A, 2E, 3A, 3E, 4A, 4E, 5A, 5E, 6A, 6E, 7A, 7E, 8A, 8E, 9A, 9E, 10A, 10E, 11A, 11E, 12A, 12E, 13A, 13E, 14A, 14E and tie off.

Tie on at 1K, pass to 1F, then 2K, 2F, 3K, 3F, 4K, 4F, 5K, 5F, 6K, 6F, 7K, 7F, 8K, 8F, 9K, 9F, 10K, 10F, 11K, 11F, 12K, 12F, 13K, 13F, 14K, 14F and tie off.
Tie on at 1J, pass to 1H, then 2J, 2H, 3J, 3H, 4J, 4H, 5J, 5H, 6J, 6H, 7J, 7H, 8J, 8H, 9J, 9H, 10J, 10H, 11J, 11H, 12J, 12H, 13J, 13H, 14J, 14H and tie off.
Tie on at 1C, pass to 1G, then 2C, 2G, 3C, 3G, 4C, 4G, 5C, 5G, 6C, 6G, 7C, 7G, 8C, 8G, 9C, 9G, 10C, 10G, 11C, 11G, 12C, 12G, 13C, 13G, 14C, 14G and tie off.
Tie on at 1D, pass to 1E, then 2D, 2E, 3D, 3E, 4D, 4E, 5D, 5E, 6D, 6E, 7D, 7E, 8D, 8E, 9D, 9E, 10D, 10E,

11D, 11E, 12D, 12E, 13D, 13E, 14D, 14E and tie off.
Tie on at 1L, pass to 1G, then 2L, 2G, 3L, 3G, 4L, 4G, 5L, 5G, 6L, 6G, 7L, 7G, 8L, 8G, 9L, 9G, 10L, 10G, 11L, 11G, 12L, 12G, 13L, 13G, 14L, 14G and tie off.
Tie on at 1M, pass to 1H, then 2M, 2H, 3M, 3H, 4M, 4H, 5M, 5H, 6M, 6H, 7M, 7H, 8M, 8H, 9M, 9H, 10M, 10H, 11M, 11H, 12M, 12H, 13M, 13H, 14M, 14H and tie off.

Diagram on page 72

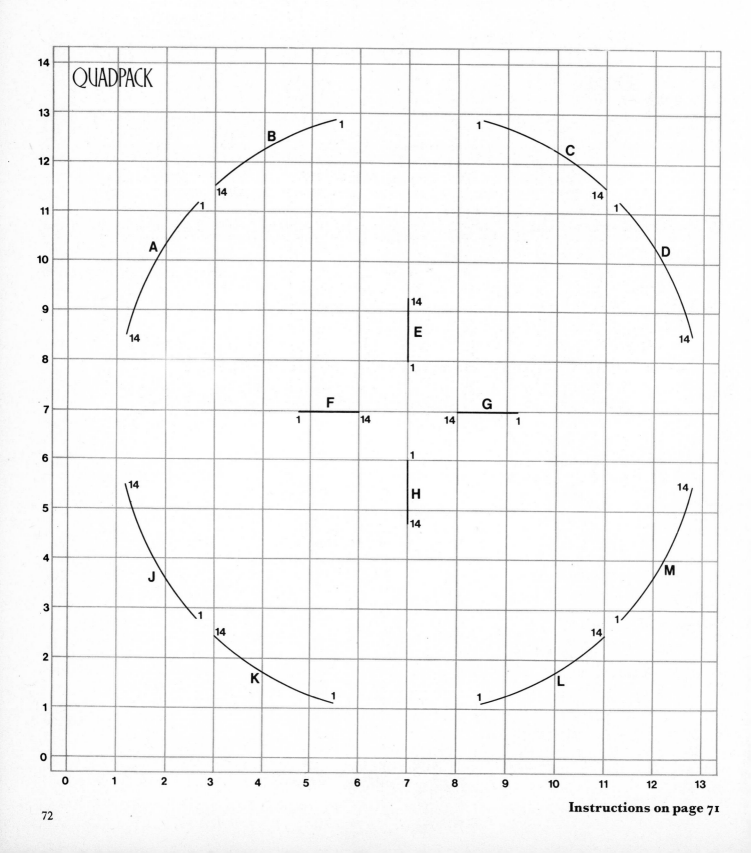

QUADPACK

Instructions on page 71

Instructions on page 76

QUINPACK

You will need

Chipboard 86.25cm (34½in) × 20cm (8in), velvet 91.25cm (36½in) × 25cm (10in), 272 panel pins, gold thread and one sheet of 2.5cm (1in) squared graph paper.

Threading the pattern

Tie with gold at 1A, pass to 1B, then 1D, 1C, 1A, 2B, 2D, 2C, 2A, 3B, 3D, 3C, 3A, 4B, 4D, 4C, 4A, 5B, 5D, 5C, 5A, 6B, 6D, 6C, 6A, 7B, 7D, 7C, 7A, 8B, 8D, 8C, 8A, 9B, 9D, 9C, 9A, 10B, 10D, 10C, 10A, 11B, 11D, 11C, 11A, 12B, 12D, 12C, 12A, 13B, 13D, 13C, 13A, 14B, 14D, 14C, 14A, 15B, 15D, 15C, 15A, 16B, 16D, 16C, 16A, 17B, 17D, 17C, 17A and tie off.

Tie on at 1D, pass to 1E, 1G, 1F, 2D, 2E, 2G, 2F, 3D, 3E, 3G, 3F, 4D, 4E, 4G, 4F, 5D, 5E, 5G, 5F and so on in this sequence until 17F and tie off.

Tie on at 1G, pass to 1H, then 1K, 1J, 2G, 2H, 2K, 2J, 3G, 3H, 3K, 3J, 4G, 4H, 4K, 4J, 5G, 5H, 5K, 5J and so on in this sequence until 17J and tie off.

Tie on at 1K, pass to 1L, then 1N, 1M, 2K, 2L, 2N, 2M, 3K, 3L, 3N, 3M, 4K, 4L, 4N, 4M, 5K, 5L, 5N, 5M and so on in this sequence until 17M and tie off.

Tie on at 1N, pass to 1P, then 1T, 1R, 1N, 2P, 2T, 2R, 2N, 3P, 3T, 3R, 3N, 4P, 4T, 4R, 4N, 5P, 5T, 5R, 5N and so on in this sequence until 17N and tie off.

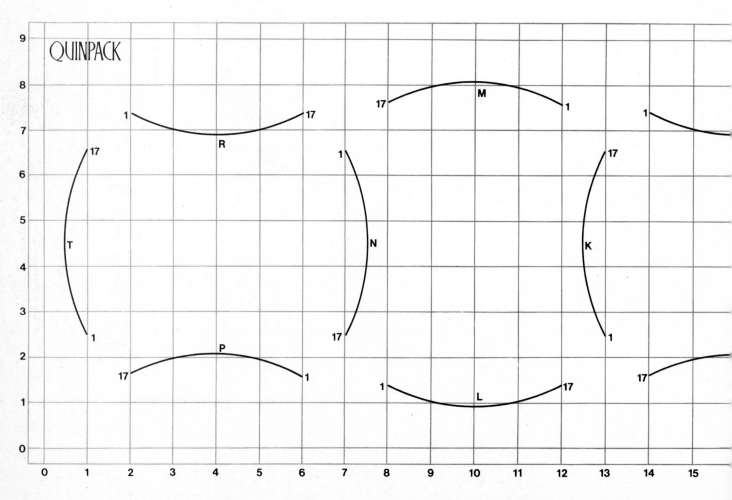

76

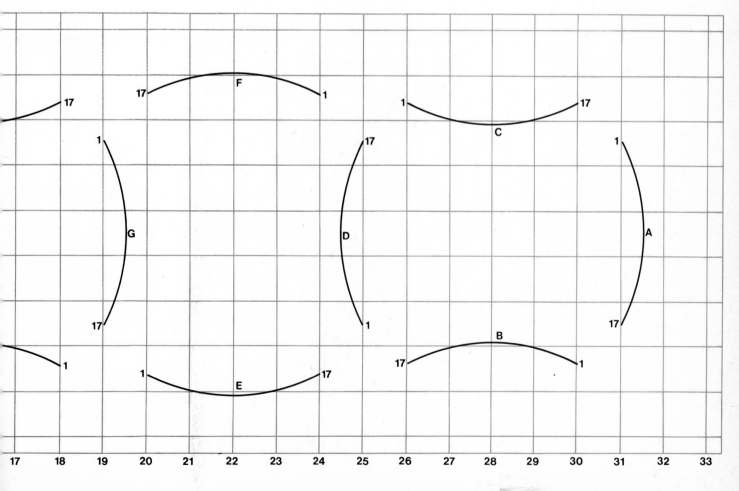

BALLERINA

You will need
Chipboard 50cm (20in) × 35cm (14in), velvet 55cm (22in) × 40cm (16in), 378 panel pins, silver and gold thread and one sheet of 2.5cm (1in) squared graph paper.

Pattern additional information
The head-dress is done by drawing lines at intervals of 2.5mm (1/10in) in direction of double ended arrows, where these lines intersect the pattern outline put a dot.

Threading the pattern
Use parallel threading for the head-dress using silver. (See chapter on parallel lines).
The eyes, eyebrows, mouth and nose are not threaded.

Dress
Section (Q)
Tie on with silver at 1Q, pass to 20Q, then 2Q, 21Q, 3Q, 22Q, 4Q, 23Q, 5Q, 24Q and so on in this sequence until 1Q again and tie off.

Section (P)
Tie on at 1P, pass to 17P, then 2P, 18P, 3P, 19P, 4P, 20P, 5P, 21P, 6P, 22P and so on in this sequence until 1P again and tie off.

Section (N)
Tie on at 1N, pass to 14N, then 2N, 15N, 3N, 16N, 4N, 17N, 5N, 18N, 6N, 19N and so on in this sequence until 1N again and tie off.

Section (F, G)
Tie on at 1G, pass to 12F, then 2G, 13F, 3G, 14F, 4G, 15F, 5G, 16F, 17F and tie off.

Section (H, J)
Tie on at 1H, then pass to 2J, then 2H, 3J, 3H, 4J, 4H, 5J, 5H, 6J, 6H and so on in this sequence until 12H and tie off.

Section (D)
Tie on at 1D, pass to 24D, then 2D, 23D, 3D, 22D, 4D, 21D, 5D, 20D, 6D, 19D and so on in this sequence until 13D and tie off.

Section (B)
Tie on at 1M, pass to 7B, then 2M, 6B, 3M, 5B, 4M, 4B, 5M, 3B, 6M, 2B, 7M, 1B, 8M, 11H, 9B, 10H, 8B, 9H, 7B, 8H and tie off.

Section (C)
Tie on at 4E, pass to 12D, then 5E, 13D, 6E, 14D, 7E, 15D, 8E, 16D, 15M, 17D, 16M, 18D, 17M, 19D, 18M, 20D, 19M, 21D, 20M, 22D, 21M, 23D, 22M, 24D and tie off.

Strap (E)
Tie on at 1E, pass to 2E, then 3E, 4E and tie off.

Strap (A, K)
Tie on at 4K, pass to 32A, then 9B and tie off.

Shoe strap (X)
Tie on at 4X, pass to 3X, then 1X, 2X, 4X, 7X, 6X, 5X, 4X and tie off.

Shoe (W)
Tie on at 1W, pass to 18W, then 2W, 17W, 3W, 16W, 4W, 15W, 5W, 14W, 6W, 13W, 7W, 12W, 8W, 11W, 9W, 10W and tie off.

Shoe (T)
Tie on at 21T, pass to 2T, then 1T, 22T, 21T, 5T, 6T, 20T, 17T, 16T, 3T, 2T, 17T, 16T, 14T, 30T, 13T, 29T, 12T, 28T, 11T, 27T, 10T, 26T, 9T, 25T, 8T, 24T, 7T, 23T and tie off.

Body outline
Tie on with gold at 1A, pass to 2A, 3A, 4A, 5A, 6A and so on in this sequence until 32A and tie off.
Use this method of threading for the remainder of the outline i.e. Lines 1R to 1T, 1S to 22T, 1U to 1X, 2X to 18W, 1W to 5X, 3X to 1V, 1F to 17F, 17F to 8H, 1M to 22M, 12D to 1D, 1L to 7L, 1K to 5K, 32A to 9B.

Diagram on page 80

BALLERINA

KNIGHT

You will need
Single knight Chipboard 50cm (20in) × 35cm (14in), velvet 55cm (22in) × 40cm (16in), 580 panel pins.
Two knights Chipboard 70cm (28in) × 35cm (14in), velvet 75cm (30in) × 40cm (16in), 1160 panel pins.
1 sheet of 2.5cm (1in) squared graph paper.

Pattern additional information
The bulk of this pattern consists of simple parallel threading so it is necessary to mark the pattern in all the areas where a double ended arrow appears. In each case mark a line in the direction of the double ended arrow and where this line strikes the pattern outline mark a dot. Then at intervals of 3.75mm (3/20in) (1½ small squares) draw lines parallel to the double ended arrow lines and where these strike the pattern outline mark a dot. Repeat for all areas with double ended arrows in them.

Threading the pattern
Use parallel threading in all areas where double ended arrows appear, thread in the direction of the arrows. (See chapter on parallel lines and use photograph for reference). Use the following colour code. Horse-brown thread. Hooves-silver thread. Saddle-turquoise thread. Knight-silver thread.
The shield and horse blanket are threaded by using gold for four pins, then green for the next four pins and so on in this sequence until the area is completed.

Plume
Tie on with green at 1B, pass to 1A, then 2B, 2A, 3B, 3A, 4B, 4A, 5B, 5A, and so on in this sequence until 15A and tie off.
Tie on with gold at 1B, pass to 1C, then 2B, 2C, 3B, 3C, 4B, 4C, 5B, 5C and so on in this sequence until 15C and tie off.

Horses ears
Tie on with brown at 1J, pass to 6J, then 2J, 7J, 3J, 8J, 4J, 9J, 5J, 10J, then 10J, 9J, 8J, 7J, 6J, 5J, 4J, 3J, 2J, 1J and tie off.
Tie on at 6K, pass to 3K, then 5K, 2K, 4K, 1K, then 2K, 3K, 4K, 5K, 6K and tie off.

Knight
Tie on with silver at 1L, pass to 9L, then 2L, 10L, 3L, 11L, 4L, 12L, 5L, 13L, 6L, 14L, 7L, 15L, 8L, 16L, 9L, 1L and tie off.
Tie on at 1G, pass to 18G, then 2G, 19G, 3G, 20G, 4G, 21G, 5G, 22G, 6G, 23G, 7G, 24G, 8G, 25G, 9G, 26G, 10G, 27G, 11G, 28G, 12G, 29G 13G, 13F, 14G, 12F, 15G, 11F, 16G, 10F, 17G, 9F, 18G, 8F and tie off.
Tie on at 1F, pass to 8F, then 2F, 9F, 3F, 10F, 4F, 11F, 5F, 12F, 6F, 13F, 7F and tie off.
Tie on at 19E, pass to 22E, then 18E, 23E, 17E, 24E, 16E, 25E, 15E, 26E, 14E, 27E, 13E, 28E, 12E, 29E, 11E and so on in this sequence until 1E and tie off.
Tie on at 1D, pass to 7D, then 2D, 8D, 3D, 9D, 4D, 10D, 5D, 11D, 6D, 12D, 7D, 1D and tie off.

Horse bridle
Tie on with turquoise at 2M, pass to 10J, then 2M, 3M, 2M, 1M, 4M, 1M, 2M and tie off.

Lance
Tie on with gold at 1H, pass to 8H, then 15H, 2H, 9H, 16H, 3H, 10H, 17H, 4H, 11H, 18H, 5H, 12H, 19H and so on in this sequence until 1H again then pass to 7H, then Z, 8H, Z, 9H and tie off. Tie on at 1X, pass to 2X, then 1X, 2X, 1X and tie off.

Horse outline
Tie on with brown at 2J, then passing from pin to pin follow outline of the horse.
Repeat for other knight but use different colours for shield and horse blanket.

Diagram on page 82–83

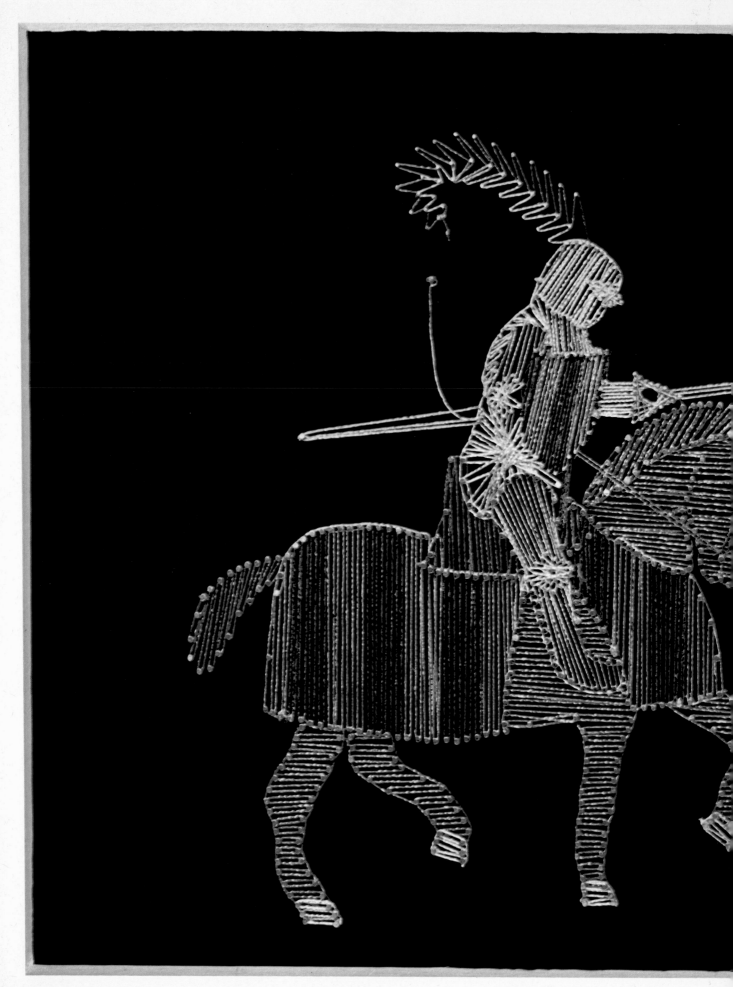

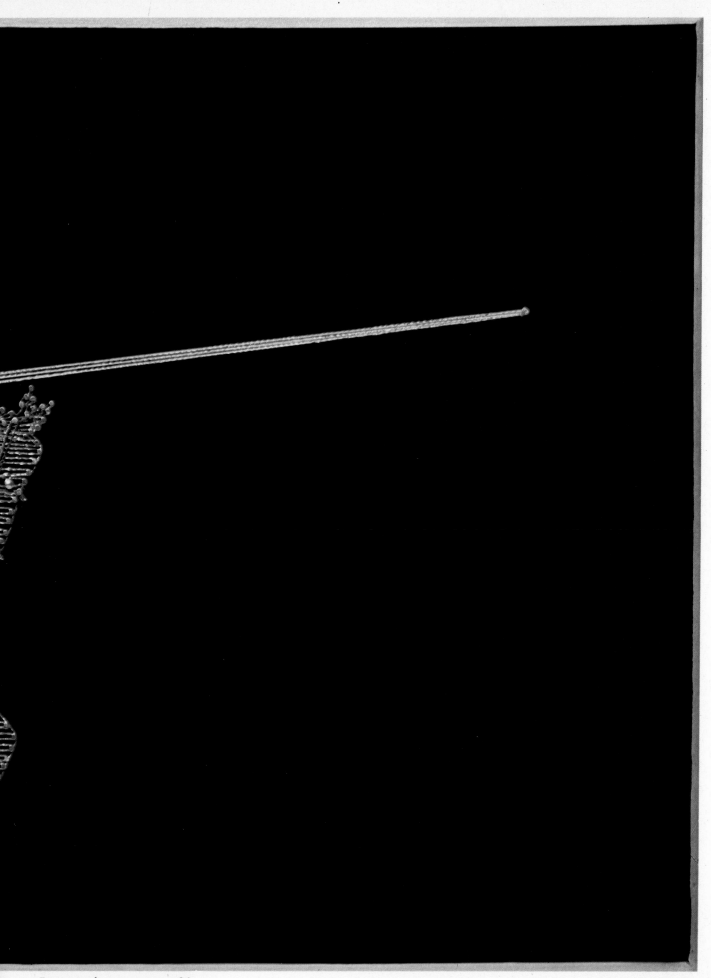

Instructions on page 81

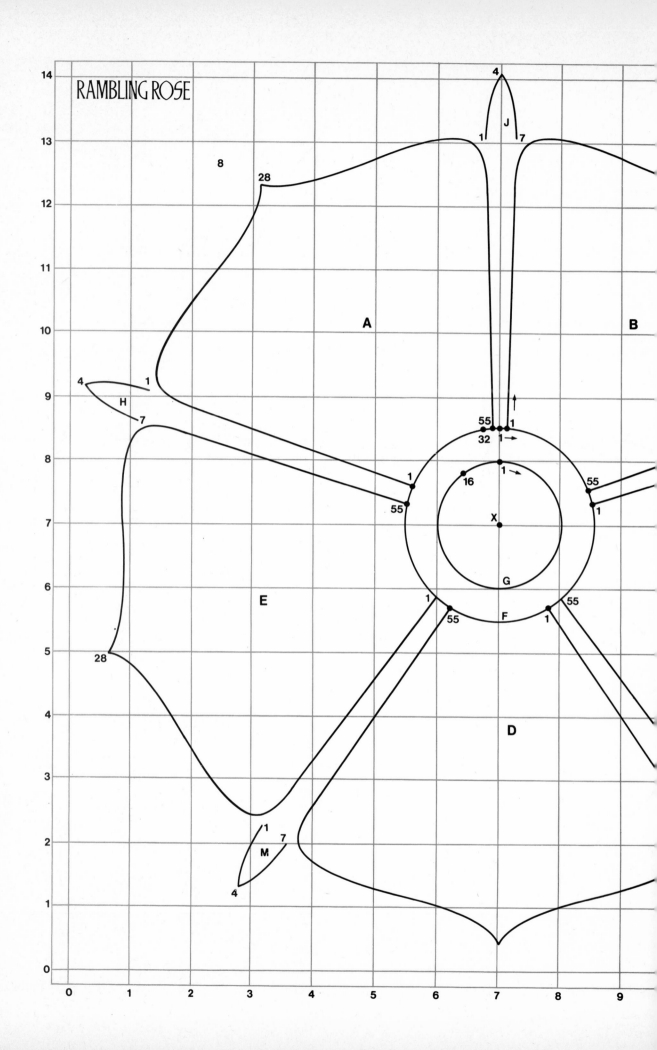

RAMBLING ROSE

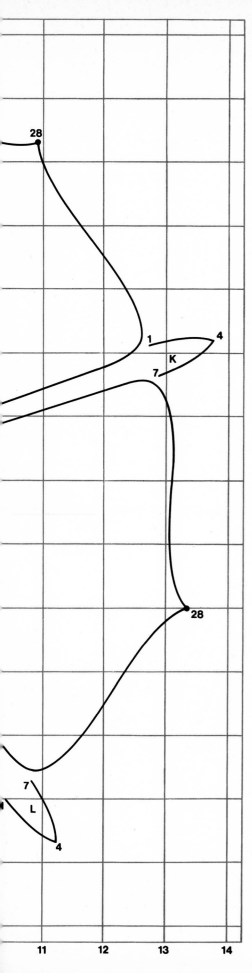

RAMBLING ROSE

You will need
Chipboard 40cm (16in) × 40cm (16in), velvet 45cm (18in) × 45cm (18in), 359 panel pins, red, green, silver and gold thread and one sheet of 2.5cm (1in) squared graph paper.

Threading the pattern
Tie on with green at X, pass to 1J, then X, 2J, X, 3J, X, 4J, X, 5J, X, 6J, X, 7J, X and tie off.
Repeat for sections K, L, M and H.
Tie on with red at 28B, pass to 4F, then 29B, 3F, 30B, 2F, 31B, 1B, 32B, 2B, 33B, 3B, 34B, 4B, 35B, 5B, 36B, 6B, 37B, 7B, 38B, 8B, 39B, 9B and so on in this sequence until 28B again and tie off.
Repeat for C, D, E and A.
Tie on with silver at 1F, pass to 10F, then 2F, 11F, 3F, 12F, 4F, 13F, 5F, 14F, 6F, 15F and so on in this sequence until 1F again and tie off.
Tie on with gold at 1G, pass to 9G, then 2G, 10G, 3G, 11G, 4G, 12G, 5G, 13G, 6G, 14G, 7G, 15G, 8G, 16G, 9G, 1G and tie off.

Instructions on page 87

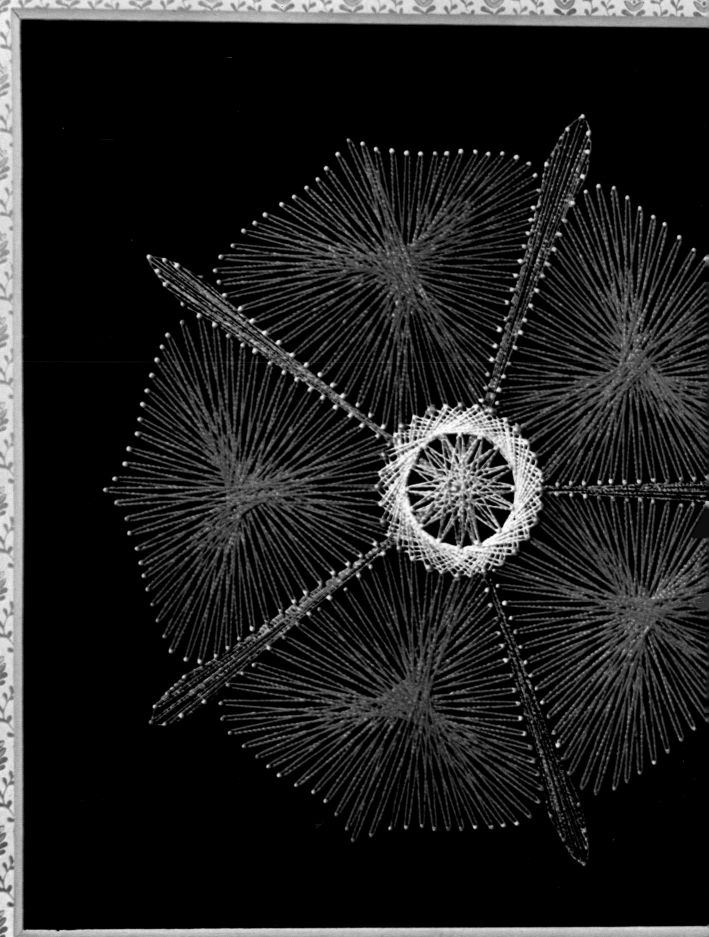

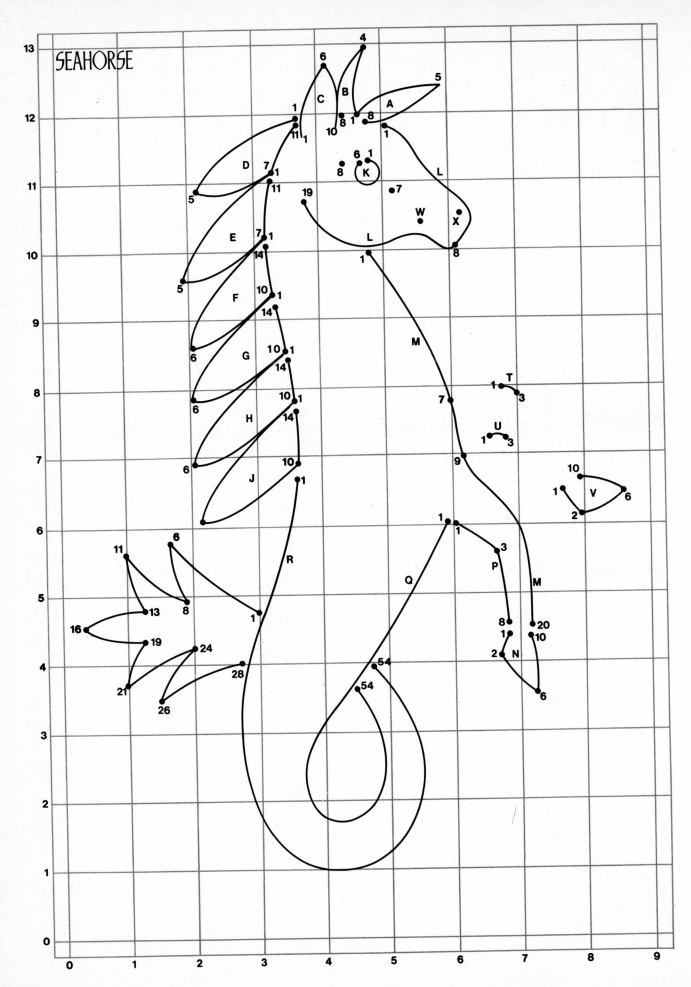

SEAHORSE

Instructions on page 92

SEAHORSE

You will need
Chipboard 35cm (14in) × 25cm (10in), velvet 40cm (16in) × 30cm (12in), 322 panel pins, 1 large headed gold coloured panel pin, gold and silver thread and one sheet of 2.5cm (1in) squared graph paper.

Threading the pattern
Knock the large headed gold coloured pin in at X.
Tie on with silver at 1A, pass to 5A, then 2A, 6A, 3A, 7A, 4A, 8A, then pass to 1B, then 5B, 2B, 6B, 3B, 7B, 4B, 8B and then pass to 10C, then 5C, 9C, 4C, 8C, 3C, 7C, 2C, 6C, 1C and tie off. Tie on at 1D, pass to 7D, then 2D, 8D, 3D, 9D, 4D, 10D, 5D, 11D, 6D, 1D and tie off.
Repeat for E.

Tie on at 1F, pass to 8F, then 2F, 9F, 3F, 10F, 4F, 11F, 5F, 12F, 6F, 13F, 7F, 14F, 8F, 1F and tie off.
Repeat for G, H and J.
Tie on at 8A, pass to 1L, then 2L, 3L, 4L and so on in this sequence until 8L, then W, 8L, 9L, 10L, 11L, 12L, 13L, 14L, 15L, 16L, 17L, 18L, 19L and tie off. Tie on at 1K, pass to 4K, then 2K, 5K, 3K, 6K, 4K, 1K, then 7K, 4K, 8K, 1K and tie off. Tie on at 1M, pass to 2M, 3M, 4M, 5M, 6M and so on until 20M, pass to 10N, then 5N, 9N, 4N, 8N, 3N, 7N, 2N, 6N, 1N, pass to 8P, then 7P, 6P, 5P, 4P, 3P, 2P, 1P and tie off. Tie on at 7M, pass to 1T, then 2T, 3T, 10V, 5V, 9V, 4V, 8V, 3V, 7V, 2V, 6V, 1V, then 3U, 2U, 1U, 9M and tie off.

Fish tail section
Tie on with gold at 1S, pass to 15S, then 2S, 16S, 3S, 17S, 4S, 18S, 5S, 19S, 6S, 20S and so on in this sequence until 28S and tie off.
Tie on at 1Q, pass to 1R, then 2Q, 2R, 3Q, 3R, 4Q, 4R, 5Q, 5R, 6Q, 6R, 7Q, 7R and so on in this sequence until 54R and tie off.

Diagram on page 90

FISH

You will need
Chipboard 37.5cm (15in) × 25cm (10in), velvet 42.5cm (17in) × 30cm (12in), 310 panel pins, red, silver, gold and turquoise thread and one sheet of 2.5cm (1in) squared graph paper.

Threading the pattern
Top fin (R)
Tie on with gold at 1R, pass to 21R, then 2R, 22R, 3R, 23R, 4R, 24R, 5R, 25R, 6R, 26R, 7R, 27R, 8R, 28R, 9R, 29R, 10R, 30R and so on in this sequence until 40R and tie off.

Bottom fin (T)
Tie on with gold at 1T, pass to 24T, then 2T, 25T, 3T, 26T, 4T, 27T, 5T, 28T, 6T, 29T, 7T, 30T, 8T, 31T, 9T, 32T, 10T, 33T and so on in this sequence until 46T and tie off.

Tail fin (S)
Tie on with gold at 1S, pass to 16S, then 2S, 17S, 3S, 18S, 4S, 19S, 5S, 20S, 6S, 21S, 7S, 22S, 8S, 23S, 9S, 24S, 10S, 25S and so on in this sequence until 30S and tie off.

Trailer (U)
Tie on with gold at 1U, pass to 2U, then 3U, 4U, 5U, 6U and tie off.

Trailer (V)
Tie on with gold at 1V, pass to 2V, then 3V, 4V, 5V, 6V, 7V and tie off.

Body (A, B, C, D, E, F, G, H, J, K, L, M & N)
Tie on with turquoise at 1A, pass to 2B, then 3A, 4B, 5A, 6B, 7A, 8B, 9A, 10B, 11A, then pass to 11B, then 10C, 9B, 8C, 7B, 6C, 5B, 4C, 3B, 2C, 1B, then 1C and so on in this sequence until N is completed.
Tie on with silver at 1B, pass to 2A, then 3B, 4A, 5B, 6A, 7B, 8A, 9B, 10A, 11B, 11C, 10B, 9C, 8B, 7C, 6B, 5C, 4B, 3C, 2B, 1C and so on in this sequence until N is completed.
Pass silver thread around the full body outline.

Eye (P)
Tie on with red at 1P, pass to 4P, then 2P, 5P, 3P, 6P, 4P, 7P, 5P, 8P, 6P, 9P, 7P, 1P, 8P, 2P, 9P, 3P, 1P, 4P and tie off.

Centre fin (Q)
Tie on with gold at 1Q, pass to 10Q, then 2Q, 11Q, 3Q, 12Q, 4Q, 13Q, 5Q, 14Q, 6Q, 15Q, 7Q, 16Q, 8Q, 17Q, 9Q, 18Q and tie off.

Diagram on page 94

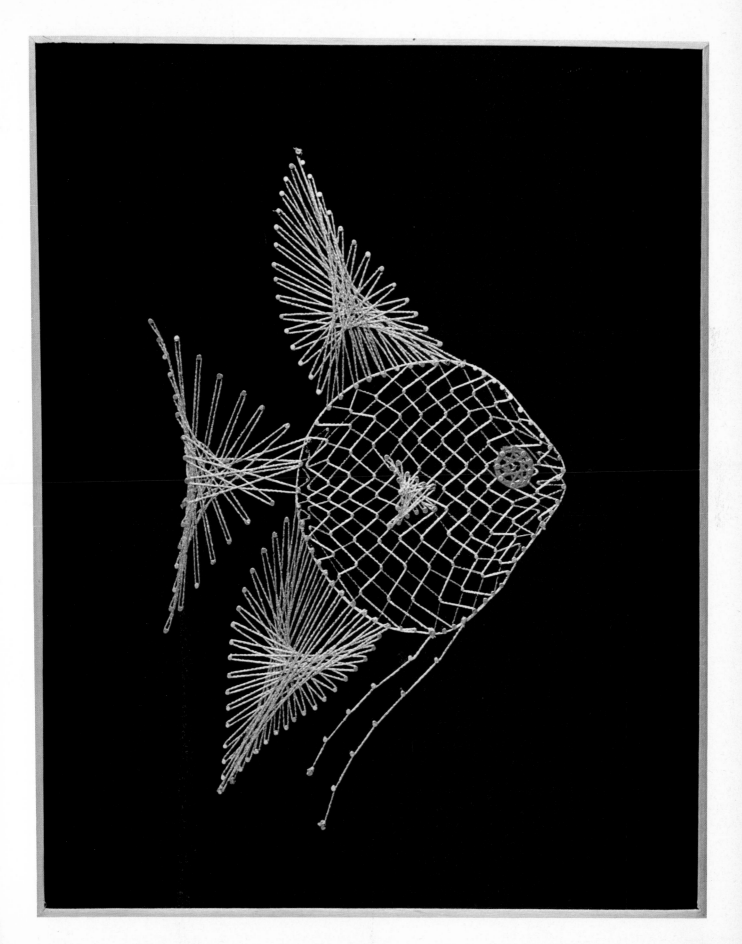

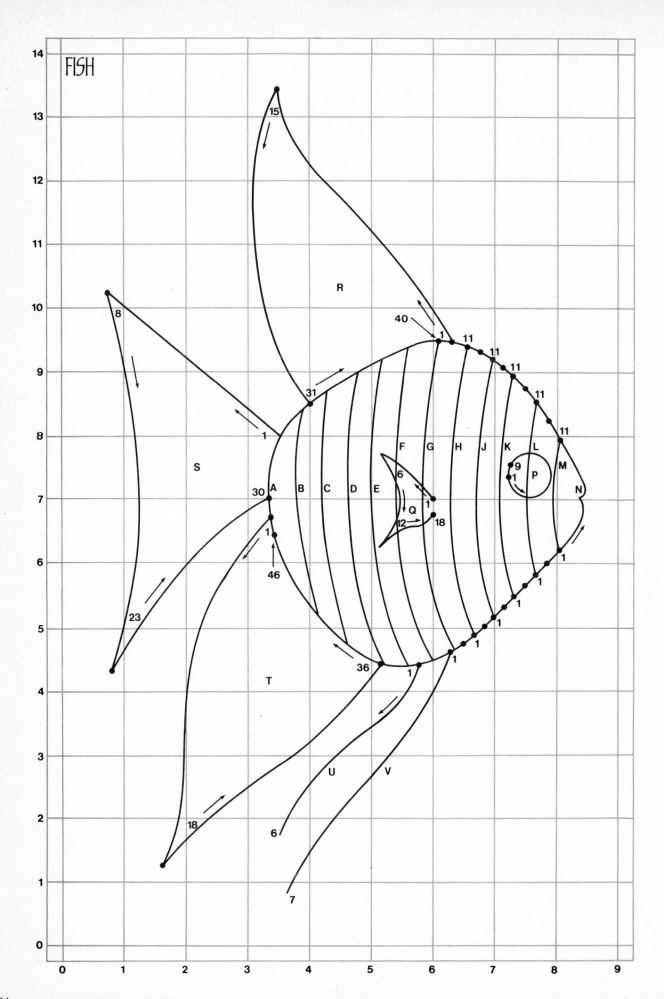

FISH

VINTAGE CAR

You will need
Chipboard 40cm (16in) × 27.5cm (11in), velvet 45cm (18in) × 32.5cm (13in), 232 panel pins, orange, silver, red, blue, gold and brown thread and one sheet of 2.5cm (1in) squared graph paper.

Threading the pattern
Body
Tie on with blue at 5F, pass to 1A, then 6F, 2A, 7F, 3A, 8F, 4A, 9F, 5A, 10F, 6A, 11F, pass to 1E, then 12F, 2E, 13F, 3E, 14F, 4E, 15F, 5E, 16F, 6E, 17F, 7E, 18F, 8E, 19F, 9E, 20F, 10E and tie off.
Tie on at 1C, pass to 10D, then 2C, 9D, 3C, 8D, 4C, 7D, 5C, 6D, 6C, 5D, 7C, 4D, 8C, 3D, 9C, 2D, 10C, 1D, 20C, 11C, 19C, 12C, 18C, 13C, 17C, 14C and tie off. Tie on at 11B, pass to 7A, then 10B, 8A, 9B, 9A, 8B, 10A, 7B, 11A, 6B, 12A, 5B, 13A, 4B, 14A, 3B, 15A, 2B, 16A, 25A, 17A, 24A, 18A, 23A, 19A and tie off.
Tie on with silver at 1F, pass to 24F, then 2F, 23F, 3F, 22F, 4F, 21F, 5F, 20F, 21F, 26F, 22F, 25F, 23F and tie off.

Mudguard
Tie on with red at 1N, pass to 2N, then 3N, 4N, 5N, 6N, 7N, 8N, 9N, 10N, 1M, 2M, 3M, 4M, 5M, 6M, 7M, 8M, 9M, 10M, then back again on the other side of the nails.

Handbrake (X, Y, Z,)
Tie on with orange at Z, pass to Y, then X, then Y and tie off.

Steering wheel (W)
Tie on with orange at 8E, pass to 3W, then 2W, 1W, 6W, 5W, 4W, 8E and tie off.

Front light (G)
Tie on with gold at 1G, pass to 7G, then 13G, 2G, 8G, 14G, 3G, 9G, 15G 4G, 10G, 16G, 5G, 11G, 17G, 6G, 12G, 18G, 7G, 13G, 19G and tie off.

Side light (H)
Tie on with gold at 1H, pass to 6H, then 11H, 2H, 7H, 12H, 3H, 8H, 13H, 4H, 9H, 14H, 5H, 10H, 15H, 6H, 11H, 16H and tie off.

Hard top (J)
Tie on with brown at 1J, pass to 7J, then 2J, 8J, 3J, 9J, 4J, 10J, 5J, 11J, 6J, 12J, pass to 17C, then 13J, 16C, 15C, 14J, 14C, 15J, 14C, 15J, 16J, 2B, 17J, 1B, 17J, then 22A, 17J, 21A, 16J, 21A, 20A, then 18J, 20A, 6J, 19A and tie off.

Wheel (K)
Tie on with silver at centre pin of wheel 25K, pass to 1K, then 25K, 3K, 25K, 5K, 25K, 7K, 25K, 9K, 25K, 11K, 25K, 13K, 25K, 15K, 25K, 17K, 25K, 19K, 25K, 21K, 25K, 23K, 25K and tie off.
Tie on with gold at 1K, pass to 7K, then 2K, 8K, 3K, 9K, 4K, 10K, 5K, 11K, 6K, 12K, 7K, 13K, 8K, 14K, 9K, 15K, 10K, 16K, 11K, 17K, 12K, 18K, 13K, 19K, 14K, 20K, 15K, 21K, 16K, 22K, 17K, 23K, 18K, 24K, 19K, 1K, and tie off.
Repeat this pattern sequence for Wheel L.

Diagram on page 96-97

VINTAGE CAR

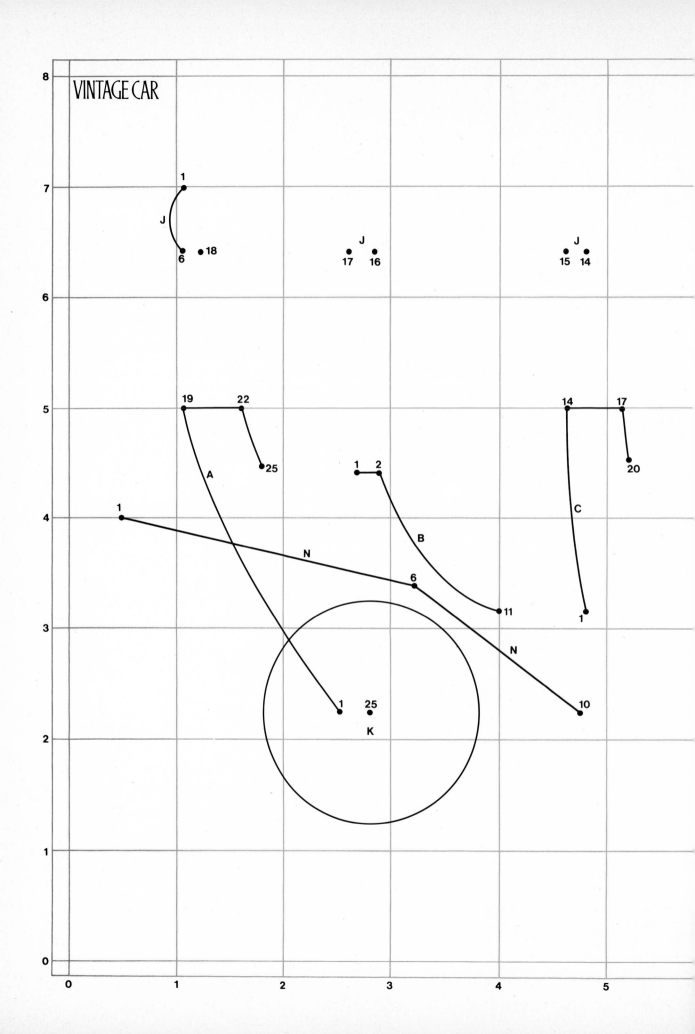

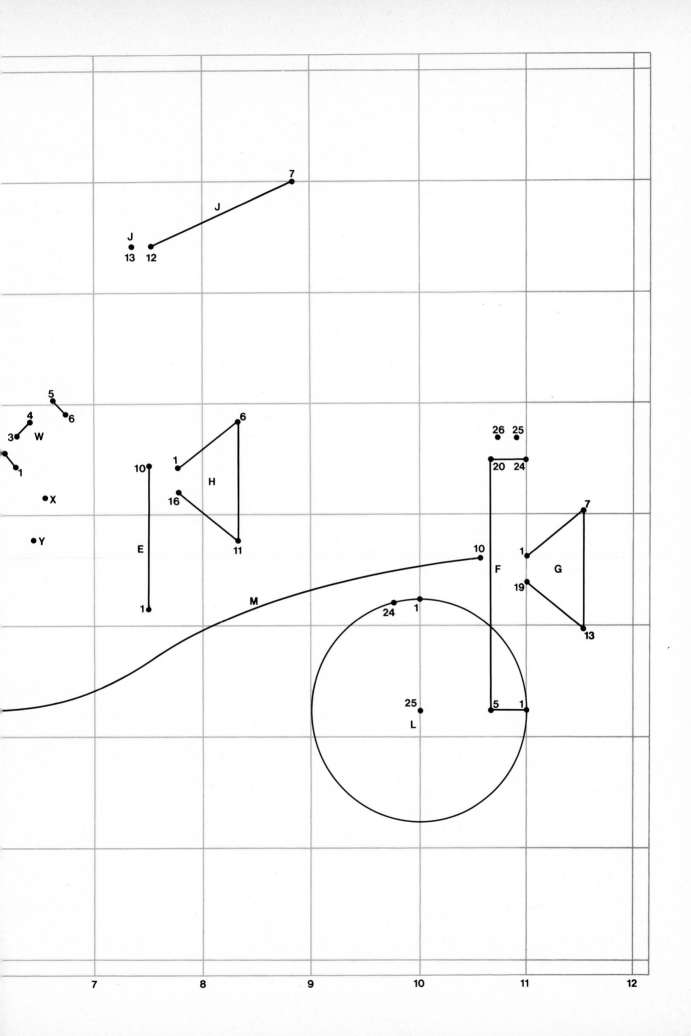

Instructions on page 95

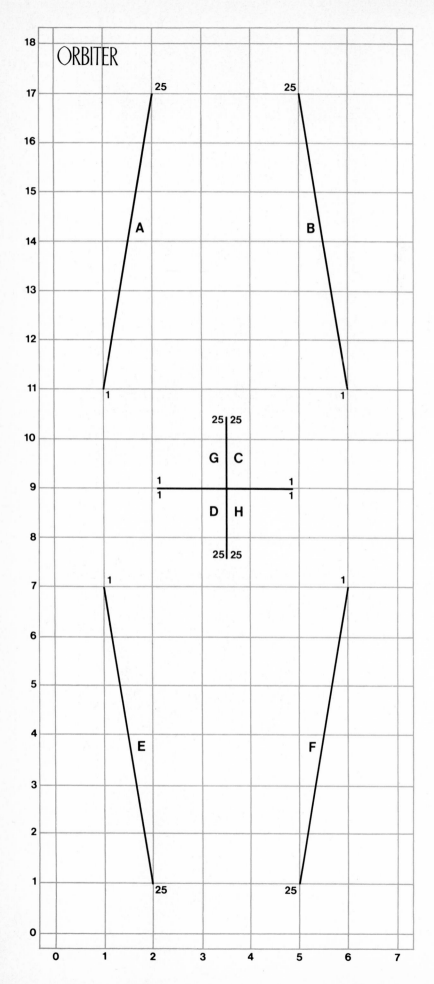

ORBITER

You will need
Chipboard 45cm (18in) × 17.5cm (7in), velvet 50cm (20in) × 22.5cm (9in), 156 panel pins, turquoise thread and one sheet of 2.5cm (1in) squared graph paper.

Threading the pattern
Tie on with turquoise at 1A, pass to 25B, then 2A, 24B, 3A, 23B, 4A, 22B, 5A, 21B, 6A, 20B, 7A, 19B, 8A, 18B, 9A, 17B, 10A, 16B, 11A, 15B, 12A, 14B, 13A, 13B, 14A, 12B, 15A, 11B, 16A, 10B, 17A, 9B, 18A, 8B, 19A, 7B, 20A, 6B, 21A, 5B, 22A, 4B, 23A, 3B, 24A, 2B, 25A, 1B and tie off.

Tie on at 1E, pass to 25F, then 2E, 24F. 3E 23F 4E, 22F, 5E, 21F, 6E, 20F, 7E, 19F, 8E and so on in this sequence until 1F and tie off.

Tie on at 1A, pass to 25G, then 2A, 24G, 3A, 23G, 4A, 22G, 5A, 21G, 6A, 20G, 7A, 19G, 8A and so on in this sequence until 1G and tie off.

Tie on at 1B, pass to 25C, then 2B, 24C, 3B, 23C, 4B, 22C, 5B, 21C, 6B, 20C, 7B, 19C, 8B and so on in this sequence until 1C and tie off.

Tie on at 1E, pass to 25D, then 2E, 24D, 3E, 23D, 4E, 22D, 5E, 21D, 6E, 20D, 7E, 19D, 8E and so on in this sequence until 1D and tie off.

Tie on at 1F, pass to 25H, then 2F, 24H, 3F, 23H, 4F, 22H, 5F, 21H, 6F, 20H, 7F, 19H, 8F and so on in this sequence until 1H and tie off.

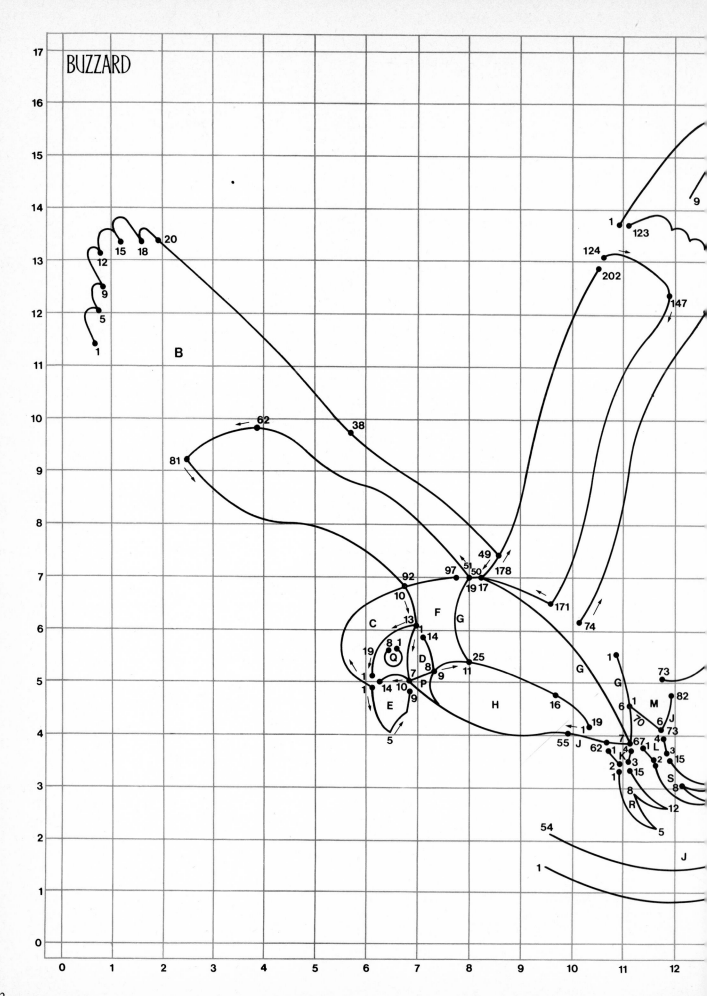

BUZZARD

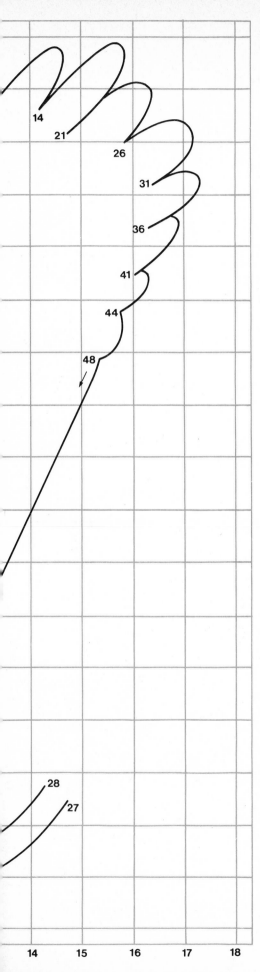

BUZZARD

You will need

Chipboard 42.5cm (17in) × 40cm (16in), velvet 50cm (20in) × 45cm (18in), 512 panel pins, brown, gold, orange, red, silver and blue thread and one sheet of 2.5cm (1in) squared graph paper.

Threading the pattern
Large wing (A)

Tie on with brown at 1A, pass to 2A, then 123A, 3A, 123A, 4A, 122A, 5A, 122A, 6A, 121A, 7A, 121A, 8A, 120A, 9A, 120A, 10A, 119A, 11A, 119A, 12A, 118A, 13A, 118A, 14A, 117A, 15A, 117A, 16A and so on in this sequence until 48A, then 99A, 49A, 98A, 50A, 97A, 51A, 96A, 52A, 95A, 53A, 94A, 54A, 93A, 55A, 92A, and so on in this sequence until 74A and tie off.

Tie on with orange at 124A, pass to 123A, 125A, 122A, 126A, 121A, 127A, 120A, 128A, 119A, 129A, 118A, 130A, 117A, 131A, 116A, 132A, 115A and so on in this sequence until 171A and tie off.

Tie on with gold at 171A, pass to 202A, then 170A, 201A, 169A, 200A, 168A, 199A, 167A, 198A, and so on in this sequence until 171A and tie off.

Small wing (B)

Tie on with brown at 1B, pass to 81B, then 2B, 81B, 3B, 80B, 4B, 80B, 5B, 79B, 6B, 79B, 7B, 78B, 8B, 78B, 9B, 77B, 10B, 77B, and so on in this sequence until 62B and tie off.

Tie on with orange at 38B, pass to 62B, then 39B, 61B, 40B, 60B, 41B, 59B, 42B and so on in this sequence until 50B and tie off.

Tie on with gold at 51B, pass to 81B, then 52B, 82B, 53B, 83B, 54B, 84B, 55B, 85B, 56B, 86B and so on in this sequence until 51B again and tie off.

Body
Section H

Tie on with silver at 1H, pass to 9H, then 2H, 10H, 3H, 11H, 4H, 12H, 5H, 13H, 6H, 14H, 7H, 15H, 8H, 16H, 9H, 1H and tie off.

Section P

Tie on with silver at 10E, pass to 9H, then 10E, 8H, 10E, 7H, 10E and tie off.

Section G

Tie on with silver at 62J, pass to 25G, then 63J, 12H, 64J, 13H, 65J, 14H, 66J, 15H, 67J and tie off.

Tie on with gold at 67J, pass to 21G, then 7G, 22G, 8G, 23G, 9G, 24G, 10G, 25G, 11G, 12H, 12G, 13H, 13G, 14H, 14G, 15H, 15G, 16H, 61J, 17H, 63J, 18H, 65J, 19H, 67J and tie off.

Tie on with gold at 6G, pass to 178A, then 5G, 177A, 4G, 176A, 3G, 175A, 2G, 174A, 1G and tie off.

Section M

Tie on with gold at 1G, pass to 82J, then 2G, 80J, 3G, 78J, 4G, 76J, 5G, 74J, 6G, 73J and tie off.

Section F

Tie on with gold at 25G, pass to 10C, then 24G, 12C, 23G, 14D, 22G, 12D, 21G, 10D, 20G, 8D, 19G and tie off.

Section C

Tie on with gold at 1C, pass to 10C, then 2C, 11C, 3C, 12C, 4C, 13C, 5C, 14C, 6C, 15C, 7C, 16C, 8C, 17C, 9C, 18C, 10C, 19C and tie off.

Section D

Tie on with brown at 1D, pass to 14D, 2D, 13D, 3D, 12D, 4D, 11D, 5D, 10D, 6D, 9D, 7D, 8D and tie off.

Beak (E)

Tie on with red at 1E, pass to 5E, then 10E, 2E, 6E, 11E, 3E, 7E, 12E, 4E, 8E, 13E, 5E, 9E, 14E, then 1E, 5E, 14E, 5E, 13E, 5E, 12E, 5E, 11E, 5E, 10E and tie off.

Continued over

Eye (Q)

Tie on with blue at 1Q, pass to 4Q, then 2Q, 5Q, 3Q, 6Q, 4Q, 7Q, 5Q, 8Q, 6Q, 1Q and tie off.

Tail (J)

Tie on with brown at 1J, pass to 54J, then 2J, 53J, 3J, 52J, 4J, 51J and so on in this sequence until 28J and tie off.

Tie on with orange at 54J, pass to 55J, then 53J, 56J, 52J, 57J, 51J, 58J, 50J, 59J, 49J and so on in this sequence until 82J and tie off.

Leg (K)

Tie on with gold at 62J, pass to 1K, then 63J, 2K, 64J, 3K, 65J, 4K, 66J and tie off.

Leg (L)

Tie on with gold at 1M, pass to 67J, then 2M, 1L, 3M, 2L, 4M, 3L, 5M, 4L, 6M, and tie off.

Claws (R and S)

Tie on with red at 1R, pass to 5R, then 2R, 6R, 3R, 7R, 4R, 8R, then 12R, 9R, 13R, 10R, 14R, 11R, 15R, 12R and tie off. Tie on at 1R, pass to 2R, then 3R, 4R, 5R, 6R and so on in this sequence until 15R and tie off. Repeat for other claw (S).

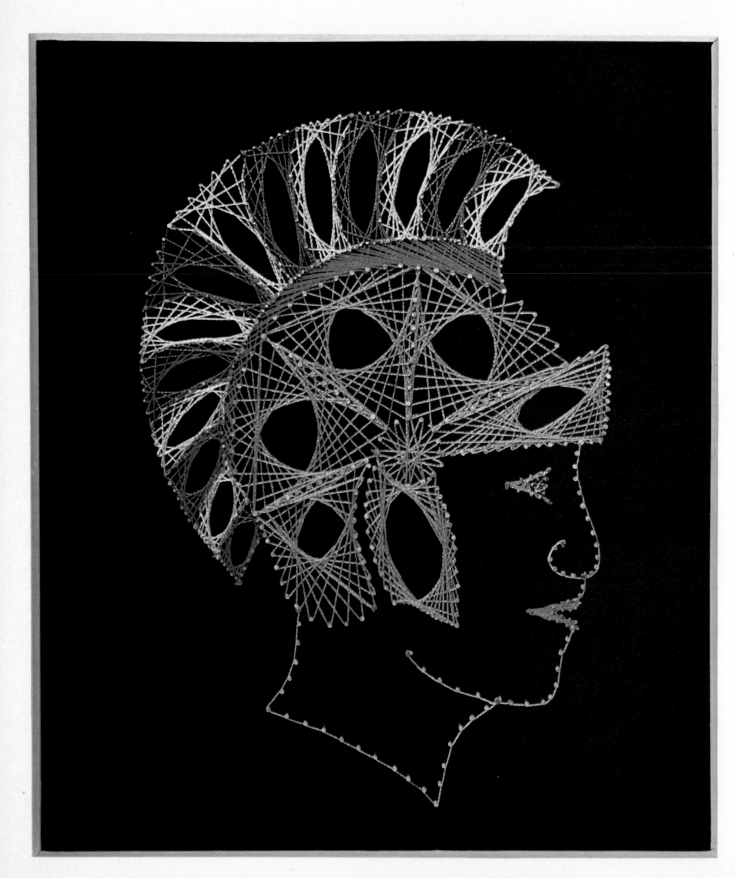

CENTURIAN

You will need
Chipboard 45cm (18in) × 35cm (14in), velvet 50cm (20in) × 40cm (16in), 575 panel pins, silver, orange, brown, green, red and gold thread and one sheet of 2.5cm (1in) squared graph paper.

Threading the pattern
Plumage (Section A)
Tie on with silver at 1A, pass to 7A, then 13A, 19A, 2A, 8A, 14A, 20A, 3A, 9A, 15A, 21A, 4A, 10A, 16A, 22A, 5A, 11A, 17A, 23A, 6A, 12A, 18A, 24A and tie off. Ensure that all thread is kept inside the four sided figure.

Repeat this pattern sequence for sections B, C, D, E, F, G, H, J, K, L, M and N.

Note Alternate silver and blue.

Tie on with red at 1X, pass to 20A, then 2X, 24B, 3X, 21B, 4X, 24C, 5X, 21C, 19S, 24D, 21S, 20D, 13R, 23E, 14R, 20E, 15R, 24F, 16R, 22F, 17R, 23G, 18R, 19G, 19R, 22H, 20R, 24J, 21R, 21J, 12Q, 22K, 13Q, 19K, 14Q, 22L, 15Q, 20L, 16Q, 23M, 17Q, 21M, 18Q, 19M, 19Q, 22N, 20Q, and tie off.

Helmet (Section S)
Tie on with orange at 1S, pass to 11S, then 21S, 2S, 12S, 22S, 3S, 13S, 23S, 4S, 14S, 24S, 5S, 15S, 25S, 6S, 16S, 26S, 7S, 17S, 27S, 8S, 18S, 28S, 9S, 19S, 29S, 10S, 20S, 30S, 11S, 21S, 31S and tie off.

Repeat this pattern for sections R and Q.

(Section V)
Tie on at 1V, pass to 12V, then 23V, 2V, 13V, 24V, 3V, 14V, 25V, 4V, 15V, 26V, 5V, 16V, 27V, 6V, 17V, 28V, 7V, 18V, 29V, 8V, 19V, 30V, 9V, 20V, 31V, 10V, 21V, 32V, 11V, 22V, 33V, 12V, 23V, 1V, and tie off.

(Section T)
Tie on at 1T, pass to 14T, then 27T, 2T, 15T, 28T, 3T, 16T, 29T, 4T, 17T, 30T, 5T, 18T, 31T and so on in this sequence until 39T, pass to 27T, 40T and tie off.

(Section W)
Tie on at 1W, pass to 12W, 25W, 37W, 2W, 13W, 26W, 37W, 3W, 14W, 27W, 38W, 4W, 15W, 28W, 38W, 5W, 16W, 29W, 39W, 6W, 17W, 30W, 39W, 7W, 18W, 31W, 40W, 8W, 19W, 32W, 40W, 9W, 20W, 33W, 41W, 10W, 21W, 34W, 41W, 11W, 22W, 35W, 42W, 12W, 23W, 36W, 42W, 13W, 24W, 37W, 1W, 14W, 25W, and tie off.

(Section U)
Tie on at 1U, pass to 9U, then 2U, 10U, 3U, 11U, 4U, 12U, 5U, 13U, 6U, 14U, 7U, 15U, 8U, 16U, 9U, 1U and tie off.

Eye (Y)
Tie on with brown at 1Y, pass to 5Y, then 2Y, 6Y, 3Y, 7Y, 4Y, 8Y, 5Y, 9Y and tie off.
Tie on with green at 10Y, pass to 14Y, then 11Y, 15Y, 12Y, 16Y, 13Y, 17Y, 14Y, 10Y and tie off.

Lips (Z)
Tie on with red at 1Z, pass to 6Z, then 2Z, 7Z, 3Z, 8Z, 4Z, 9Z, 5Z, 10Z, 6Z, 1Z and tie off.
Repeat for lip Z2.

Outline of face
Tie on with gold at 1AA, pass to 2AA, 3AA, 4AA, 5AA and so on in this sequence until the outline is complete.
i.e. Lines 1AA to 24AA, 25AA to 39AA, 40AA to 43AA, 44AA to 62AA.

Diagram on page 108

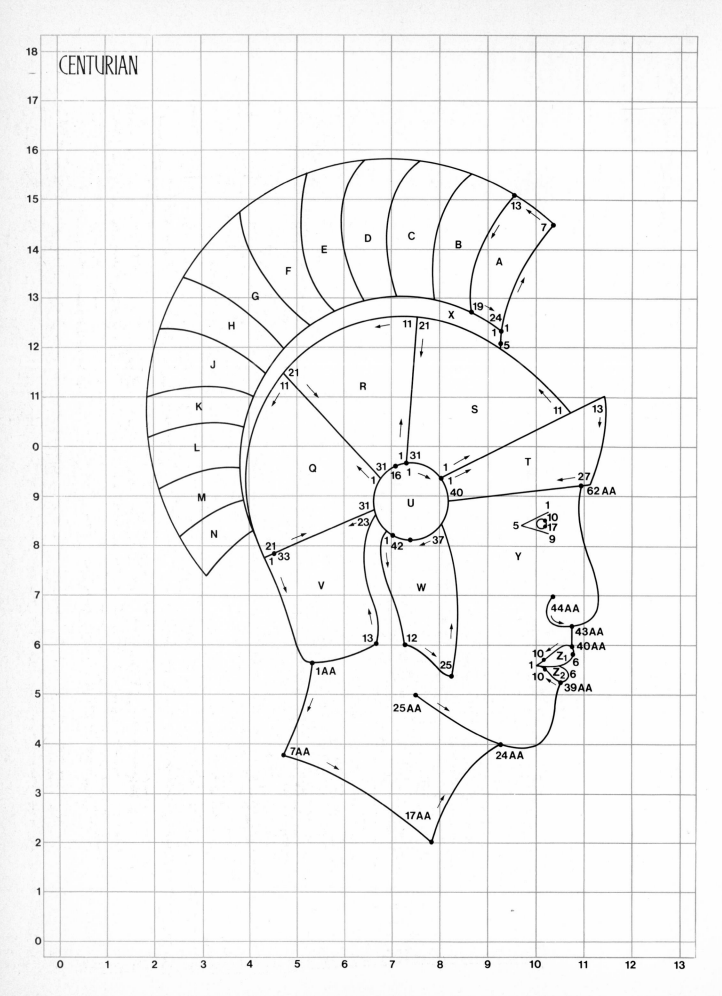

CENTURIAN

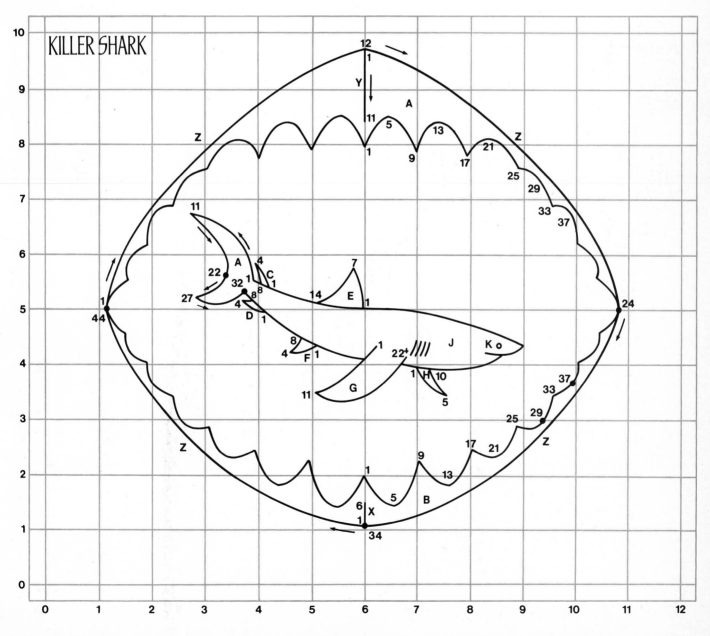

KILLER SHARK

KILLER SHARK

You will need
Chipboard 30cm (12in) × 25cm (10in), velvet 35cm (14in) × 30cm (12in), 418 panel pins, silver and turquoise thread and one sheet of 2.5cm (1in) squared graph paper.

Pattern additional information
Draw the outline of the shark only without fins, mark horizontal lines across the outline of the shark at intervals of $1\frac{1}{2}$ squares 3.75mm (3/20in) vertically and where the horizontal lines strike the outline put a dot. (See chapter on parallel lines). Now complete the rest of the pattern.

Threading the pattern
Thread shark outline as for parallel area using silver.

Fin (A)
Tie on with silver at 1A, pass to 12A, then 2A, 13A, 3A, 14A, 4A, 15A, 5A, 16A, 6A, 17A, 7A, 18A, 8A, 19A, 9A, 20A, 10A, 21A, 11A, 22A, then pass to 27A, then 23A, 28A, 24A, 29A, 25A, 30A, 26A, 31A, 27A, 32A and tie off.

Fin (C)
Tie on with silver at 1C, pass to 4C, then 2C, 5C, 3C, 6C, 4C, 7C, 5C, 8C and tie off.
Repeat this procedure for fins D and F.

Fin (E)
Tie on with silver at 1E, pass to 8E, then 2E, 9E, 3E, 10E, 4E ,11E, 5E, 12E, 6E, 13E, 7E, 14E and tie off.

Fin (G)
Tie on with silver at 1G, pass to 12G, then 2G, 13G, 3G, 14G, 4G, 15G, 5G, 16G, 6G, 17G, 7G, 18G, 8G, 19G, 9G, 20G, 10G, 21G, 11G, 22G and tie off.

Fin (H)
Tie on with silver at 1H, pass to 6H, then 2H, 7H, 3H, 8H, 4H, 9H, 5H, 9H, 6H, 10H and tie off.

Eye (K)
Knock in a large headed coloured pin to make a beady eye.

Shark teeth (B)
Tie on with silver at 5B, pass to 9B, then 6B, 10B, 7B, 11B, 8B, 12B, 9B, 13B, then 7B, 12B, 6B, 11B, 5B, then start next tooth.
Repeat this sequence for all teeth including teeth A.

Lower jaw (Z)
Tie on with turquoise at 1X, pass to 33Z, then 2X, 32Z, 3X, 31Z, 4X, 30Z, 5X, 29Z, 6X, 5B, 28Z, 13B, 27Z, 21B, 26Z, 29B, 25Z, 37B, 24Z, then pass to 25Z, 26Z, 27Z, 28Z, 29Z, 30Z, 31Z, 32Z, 33Z, 34Z and tie off.
Repeat for left hand side of lower jaw.

Upper jaw (Z)
Tie on with turquoise at 1Y, pass to 13Z, then 2Y, 14Z, 3Y, 15Z, 4Y, 16Z, 5Y, 17Z, 6Y, 18Z, 7Y, 19Z, 8Y, 20Z, 9Y, 21Z, 10Y, 22Z, 11Y, 21A, 23Z, 25A, 24Z, then 23Z, 22Z, 21Z, 20Z, 19Z, 18Z, 17Z, 16Z, 15Z, 14Z, 13Z, 12Z and tie off.
Repeat for left hand side of upper jaw.

Gills (J)
Cut silver thread into four lengths of $\frac{1}{4}$in each, glue each piece onto the the threaded area in position shown on diagram.

Diagram on page 109

Instructions on page 115

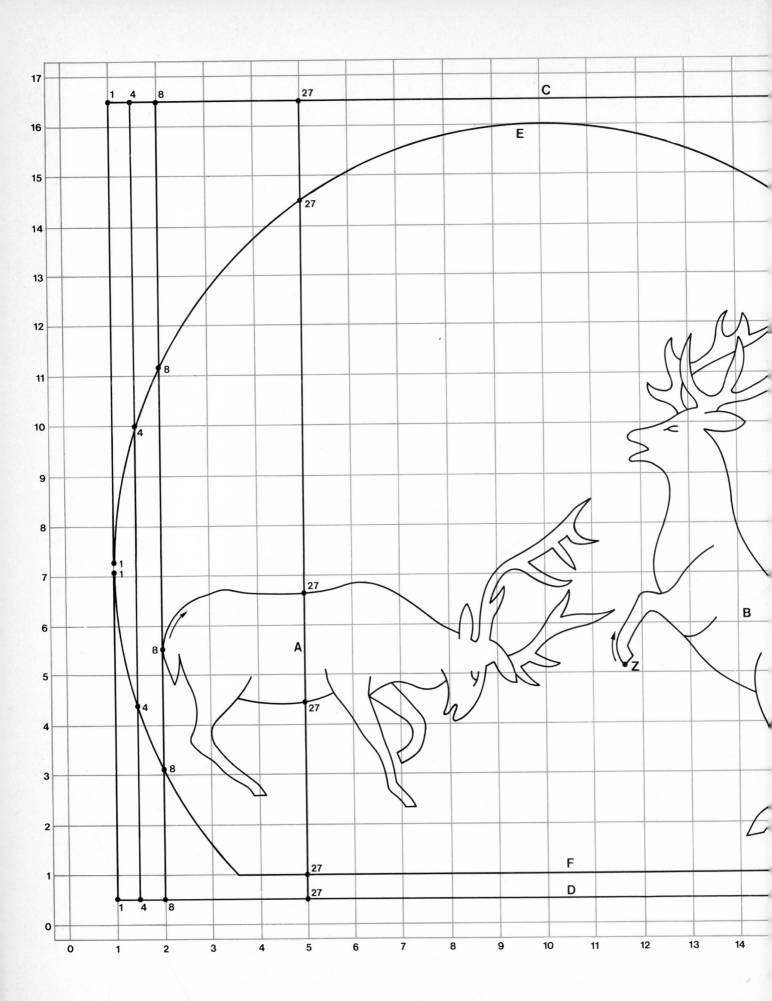

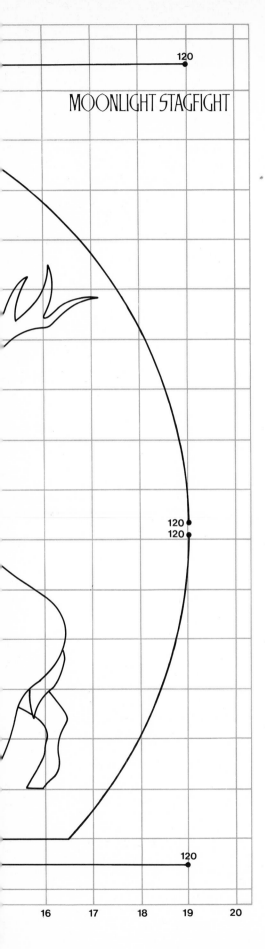

MOONLIGHT STAGFIGHT

120

120
120

120

16   17   18   19   20

MOONLIGHT STAGFIGHT

You will need
Chipboard 55cm (22in) × 45cm (18in), velvet 60cm (24in) × 50cm (20in), 812 panel pins, gold thread and one sheet of 2.5cm (1in) squared graph paper.

Pattern additional information
Divide line C into 119 equal spaces which gives 120 dots. Divide line D into 119 equal spaces which gives 120 dots.

Draw a line vertically from 1C to 1D, this should pass through the pattern outline at points 1E and 1F. Then draw lines vertically from 2C to 2D, 3C to 3D, 4C to 4D, 5C to 5D, 6C to 6D and so on until line 120C to 120D is drawn, where these vertical lines intersect the pattern outline put a dot.

Examples Line 1C to 1D passes through the pattern outline at 1E and 1F, line 4C to 4D passes through the pattern outline at 4E and 4F, line 8C to 8D passes through the pattern outline at 8E, 8A and 8F, line 120C to 120D passes through the pattern outline at 120E and 120F.

Threading the pattern
Stag A
Tie on with gold at pin 8, pass to pin 9, then pin 10, pin 11, pin 12, pin 13, pin 14 and so on in this method to complete the outline of stag A.

Stag B
Tie on with gold at pin Z, then passing from pin to pin follow the outline in the direction of the arrow until the outline is completed.

Moon outline
Tie on with gold at 1E, pass to 2E, then 3E, 4E, 5E and so on in this sequence until 120E, then 120F, 119F, 118F, 117F, 116F, 115F and so on in this sequence until 1E again and tie off.

Moon
Tie on with gold at 1E, pass to 1F, then 2E, 2F, 3E, 3F, 4E, 4F, 5E, 5F, 6E, 6F, 7E, 7F, 8E, then pin 8 on stag A, 9E, pin 9 on stag A, 10E, pin 10 on stag A and so on threading up and down right across the pattern leaving the areas enclosed by stag A and stag B unthreaded, tie on and off as necessary.

See chapter on parallel lines and use photograph for reference.

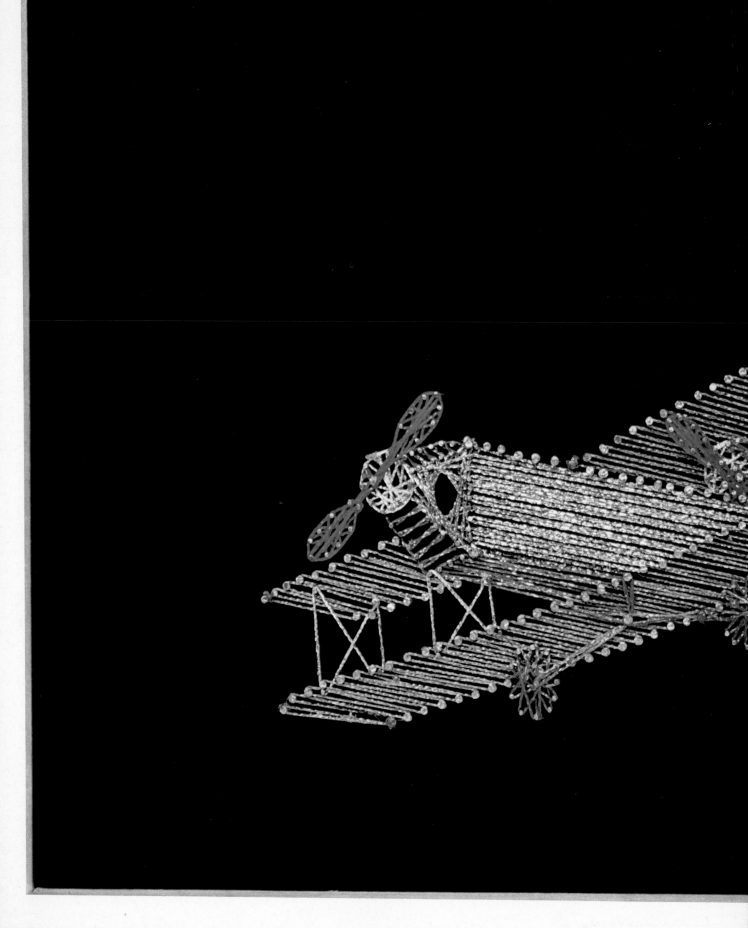

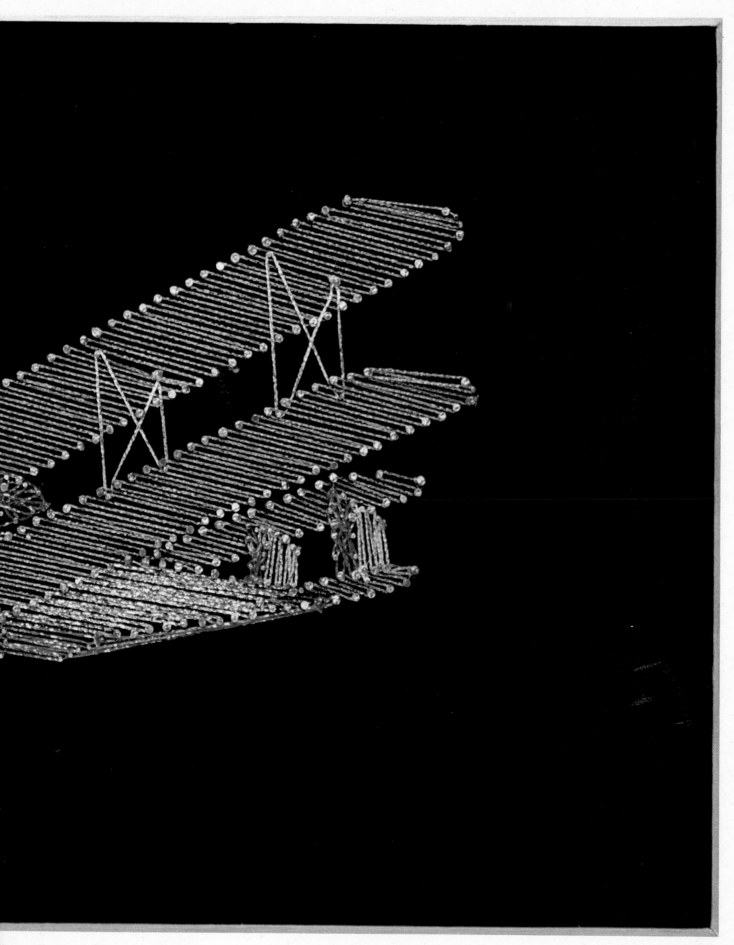

Instructions on page 120

117

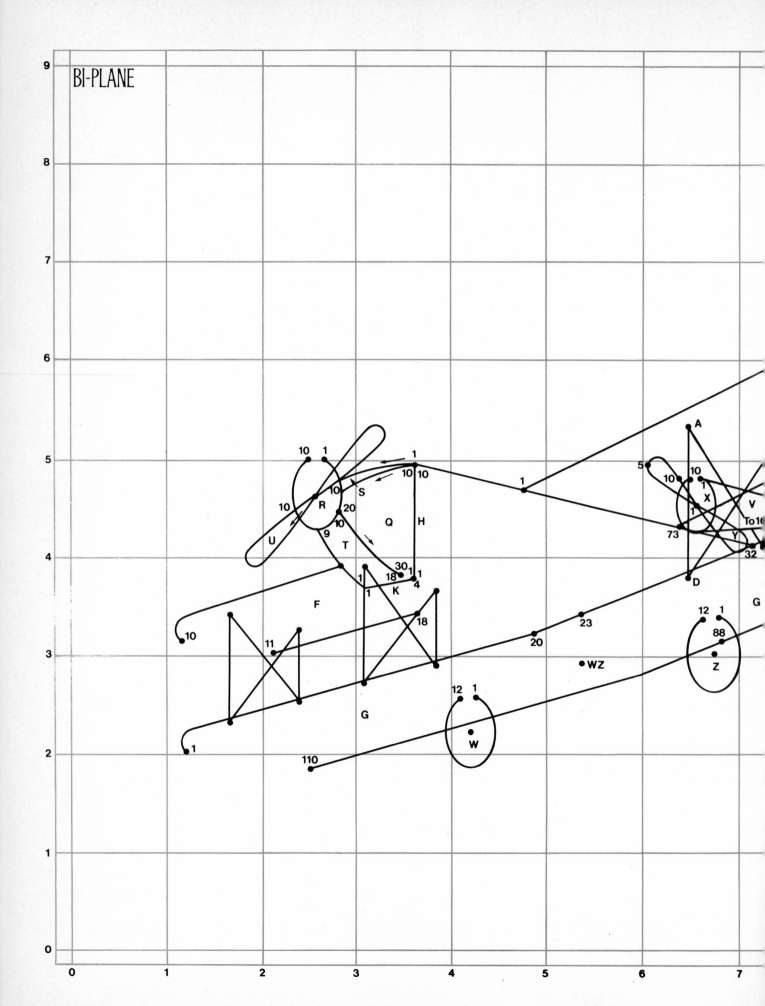

BI-PLANE

118

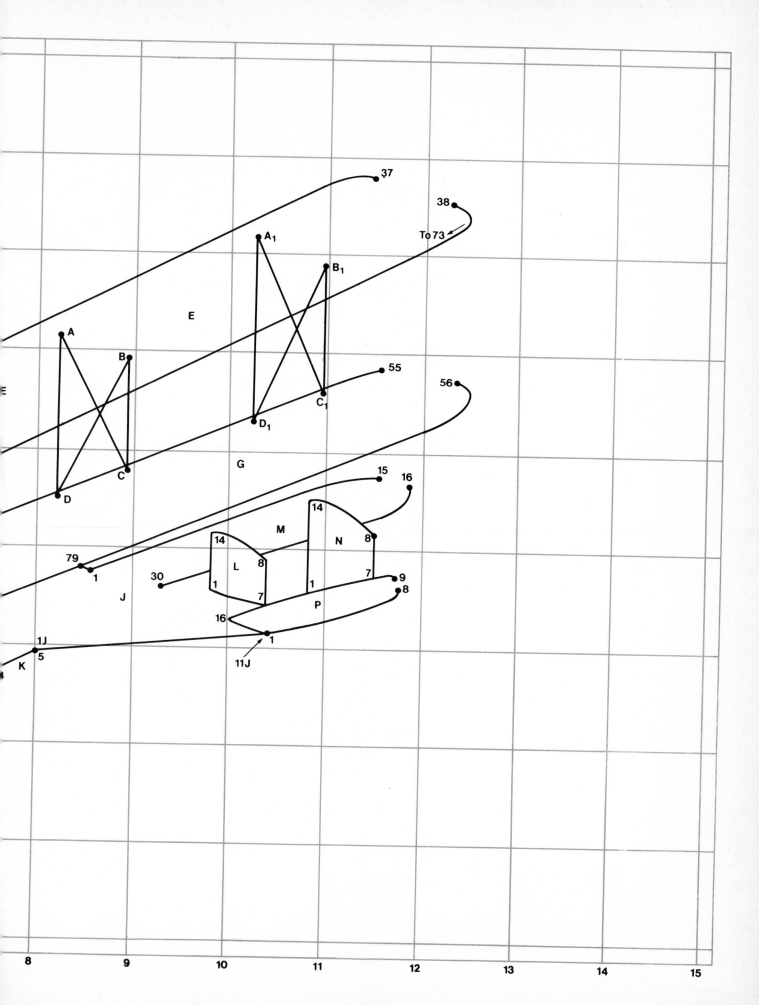

BI-PLANE

You will need

Chipboard 45cm (18in) × 30cm (12in), velvet 50cm (20in) × 35cm (14in), 506 panel pins, turquoise, gold, silver, red, brown, purple thread and one sheet of 2.5cm (1in) squared graph paper.

Threading the pattern

Wing (E)

Tie on with turquoise at 1E, pass to 73E, then 2E, 72E, 3E, 71E, 4E, 70E, 5E, 69E, 6E, 68E and so on in this sequence until 38E and tie off.

Wing (F)

Tie on with turquoise at 10F, pass to 11F, then 9F, 12F, 8F, 13F, 7F, 14F, 6F, 15F, 5F, 16F, 4F, 17F, 5F, 18F, 1F and tie off.

Wing braces (A, B, C & D)

Tie on with silver at 1A, pass to 1C, then 1B, 1D, 1A and tie off.
Repeat for other wing braces.

Wing (G)

Tie on with turquoise at 1G, pass to 110G, then 2G, 109G, 3G, 108G, 4G, 107G, 5G, 106G, 6G, 105G, 7G, 104G and so on in this sequence until 56G and tie off.

Wing (M)

Tie on with turquoise at 1M, pass to 30M, then 2M, 29M, 3M, 28M, 4M, 27M, 5M, 26M, 6M, 25M, 7M, 24M, 8M and so on in this sequence until 16M and tie off.

Wing (P)

Tie on with turquoise at 1P, pass to 16P, then 2P, 15P, 3P, 14P, 4P, 13P, 5P, 12P, 6P, 11P, 7P, 10P, 8P, 9P and tie off.

Fuselage (H)

Tie on with gold at 1H, pass to 23G, then 2H, 24G, 3H, 25G, 4H, 26G, 5H and so on in this sequence until 32G and tie off.

Fuselage (J)

Tie on with gold at 1J, pass to 88G, 2J, 87G, 3J, 86G, 4J, 85G, 5J, 84G and so on in this sequence until 79G and tie off.

Fuselage (K)

Tie on with brown at 1K, pass to 20G, then 2K, 21G, 3K, 22G, 4K, 23G and tie off. Tie on at 88G, pass to 5K, then 89G, 6K, 90G, 7K, 91G, 8K, pass to 1P, then 7K, 1P, 6K, 1P, 5K and tie off.

Wheels (W)

Tie on with purple at 1W, pass to 7W, then 2W, 8W, 3W, 9W, 4W, 10W, 5W, 11W, 6W, 12W, 1W and tie off.
Repeat for Wheel Z.

Undercarriage

Tie on with purple at centre of wheel W, pass to nail (W, Z), then 23G, nail (W, Z), 20G, nail (W, Z), 10Z, nail (W, Z), centre of wheel W and tie off.

Flap (N)

Tie on with purple at 1N, pass to 14N, then 2N, 13N, 3N, 12N and tie off.
Tie on with silver at 4N, pass to 11N, then 5N, 10N, 6N, 9N, 7N, 8N and tie off.
Repeat for Flap L.

Fuselage (T)

Tie on with brown at 1T, pass to 2T, then 17T, 16T, 3T, 4T, 15T, 14T, 5T, 6T and so on in this sequence until 9T, then 8T, 11T, 12T, 7T, 6T, 13T, 14T, 5T, 4T and so on in this sequence until 18T and tie off.

Fuselage (S)

Tie on at 1S, pass to 2S, then 11Q, 3S, 12Q, 4S, 13Q, 5S, 14Q, and so on in this sequence until 10S and tie off.

Fuselage (Q)

Tie on with gold at 1Q, pass to 10Q, then 20Q, 2Q, 11Q, 21Q, 3Q, 12Q, 22Q, 4Q, 13Q, 23Q, 5Q, 14Q, 24Q and so on in this sequence until 30Q and tie off.

Engine (V)

Tie on with brown at 1V, pass to 6V, then 2V, 7V, 3V, 8V, 4V, 9V, 5V, 10V and tie off.

Engine (X)

Tie on with silver at 1X, pass to 6X, then 2X, 7X, 3X, 8X, 4X, 9X, 5X, 10X, 1X and tie off.
Repeat for Engine Part R.

Propeller (Y)

Tie on with red at 1Y, pass to 6Y, then 2Y, 7Y, 3Y, 8Y, 4Y, 9Y, 5Y, 10Y, pass to 1Y, then repeat for other half of propeller .
Repeat above for Propeller U.

Diagram on page 118–119